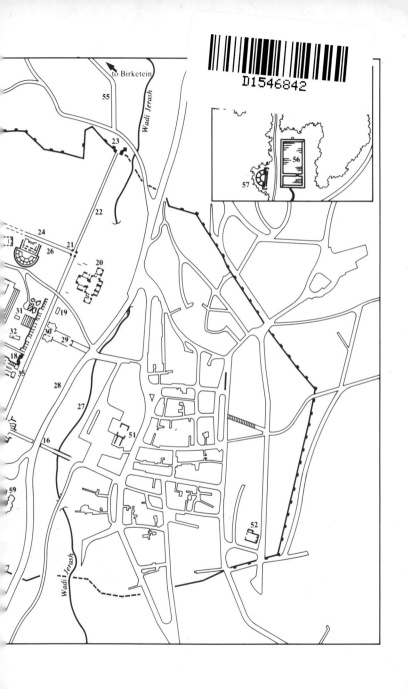

to Birketein

55

Wadi Jerash

23

22

24

21

26

20

59

31

32

19

30

29

18

35

28

27

16

51

7

Wadi Jerash

52

56

57

D1546842

JERASH

A frontier city
of the Roman East

Rami Khouri

With photographs by the author

Longman

LONDON AND NEW YORK

To the memory of
Haitham Goussous

LONGMAN GROUP LTD
Longman House
Burnt Mill, Harlow, Essex.

First published 1986
ISBN 0582 78384 4

British Library Cataloguing in Publication Data

Khouri, Rami G.
Jerash.
1. Gerasa (Ancient city)—Description—
Guide-books
I. Title
915.695'3   DS154.9.J37

ISBN 0–582–78384–4

Set in 9 on 10 point Palatino
Produced by Longman Group (FE) Limited
Printed in Hong Kong
Distributed in Jordan by
Jordan Distribution Agency

Table of Contents

Author's Preface

One of the exciting things about Jerash today, as it was during the city's days of glory nearly two millennia ago, is the blend of eastern and western cultures that is accommodated within its city walls. While Jerash welcomes tens of thousands of foreign visitors every year, it is also a major attraction for Jordanian families and schoolchildren who come regularly to enjoy an outing among the majestic ruins. Particularly on Fridays, the site is full of Jordanian and foreign visitors who come to indulge in the timeless pleasures of an ancient city – strolling through the streets or along the wide sidewalks, sitting in the theatres, climbing staircases, visiting churches, mosques, baths, tombs or houses, sipping a cool soft drink, enjoying a meal, or simply sitting in the shade of a 2nd-century AD Corinthian column and taking in the marvels of a city that has come back to life.

The Jerash Festival, the sound and light show, and the Jerash International Project, to excavate and restore major parts of the ruins, are the most important factors behind the revival of the city. This book has been conceived and produced as a practical guide to help visitors appreciate fully the monuments of ancient Jerash. It is designed to be carried around the site and read while visiting the individual monuments, with the historical outline intended to provide the background to the birth, rise, decline, abandonment and rediscovery of the city. Persons interested in further information should refer to the bibliography at the end of the book. The division of the monuments into nine groups has been done in an arbitrary manner to facilitate self-guided walking tours of the city.

I have been privileged to enjoy the kind cooperation and wise advice of many people during the research and writing of this book, and I have tried to give credit in the text to all who were so generous with their time and scholarly knowledge. This book reflects, fundamentally, the fruits of the research of hundreds of Jordanian and international archaeologists and scholars who have worked at Jerash during the past century.

In particular, I would like to express special thanks to Dr Adnan Hadidi, the Director of the Jordanian Department of Antiquities, for his personal warmth, strong support and considerable practical assistance during my work on this book, and especially for allowing me full access to the resources and personnel of the Department of Antiquities. The staff members of the Department of Antiquities' Registration Centre and Library have been consistently kind. Mrs Aida Naghwei, the Inspector of Antiquities at Jerash, and her entire staff were always gracious, generous and patient, for which they have my deep appreciation. I would also like to thank all of the international team leaders and staff members of the Jerash International Project for their time and for the substantive information they gave me. I am particularly indebted to Julian Bowsher, Jacques Seigne, Warwick Ball and John Stewart, who repeatedly suffered, but ultimately remedied, the considerable confusion I brought to bear upon them and this ancient city. Like the old stones of Jerash itself, I believe they have survived the ordeal. Working with Janet Brown, Janice Paveley, Andy Smart and all the other professionals at Longman has been, as always, a treat.

The drawings on pages 26, 59, 76 and 92 were prepared especially for this book.
All other maps and plans are by Swanston Graphics, Rugby, England.

Chronological Table

	Jerash and the Middle East	The World
332 BC	Alexander the Great conquers Syria, starts establishing Hellenistic colonies throughout the area, establishes port of Alexandria in Egypt.	In Athens, the philosopher Aristotle founds peripatetic school of philosophy.
198 BC	Seleucid King Antiochus III of Syria defeats Ptolemies of Egypt and captures region of Jordan and Palestine. Jerash formally established soon after as Hellenistic city, probably early in 2nd century BC, when it was called Antioch on the Chrysorhoas.	Rome defeats Macedonians in Second Macedonian War.
167 BC	Judas Maccabeus assumes power in Judaea after Maccabean revolt against Seleucid King Antiochus IV, and dominates Jerash and most other Decapolis cities.	Macedonians sold as slaves in Rome.
103 BC	Alexander Jannaeus takes power in Judaea, annexes Jerash to the Maccabean Kingdom in Jerusalem.	Chinese ships reach east coast of India. Gaius Julius Caesar born (100 BC).
64 BC	Roman General Pompey captures Syria and the land of the Decapolis cities, and joins them to the Roman Empire within new Roman Province of Syria. Antioch on the Chrysorhoas becomes Gerasa.	Horace, the Roman poet, born (65 BC). Florence founded (62 BC).
AD 40–70	First Roman city plan of Gerasa (Jerash) established, including city walls, Temples of Zeus and Artemis and colonnaded streets. Jews in Palestine revolt against Rome; Jerusalem destroyed (AD 70).	Nero commits suicide in Rome (AD 68). Christians first persecuted in Rome (AD 64). Gospel according to St Mark written (AD 65).

AD 106	Emperor Trajan annexes Nabataean Kingdom and reorganizes the area into a Province of Syria and a Province of Arabia. *Via Nova Traiana* built.	
AD 129–30	Emperor Hadrian visits Jerash; Hadrian's Arch built at Jerash.	Hadrian's Wall built in Great Britain (AD 122-217).
AD 211–17	During reign of Emperor Caracalla, Jerash's status raised to that of colony, named Colonia Aurelia Antoniniana.	Baths of Caracalla built in Rome.
AD 286	Emperor Diocletian rules eastern half of Roman Empire, reviving fortunes of Jerash and other Greco–Roman cities by re-establishing security, and reforming army and economic and political system. Borders of Province of Arabia changed: south pulled back to Wadi Hasa, while north extended to Hawran.	Christianity spreading quickly throughout Empire.
AD 330	Church of the Nativity built in Bethlehem (AD 325).	Emperor Constantine dedicates Constantinople as the 'New Rome', and capital of Byzantine Empire.
AD 527–65	Emperor Justinian briefly revives fortunes of Jerash; many Byzantine churches built in the city. Church of the Nativity rebuilt in Bethlehem (AD 565).	Work begins on St Sophia Basilica, Constantinople (AD 537). Europe and Britain suffer from the plague.
AD 614–30	Persians occupy Jerash.	Porcelain produced in China.
AD 636	Islamic army defeats forces of Byzantium at Yarmouk. Jerash falls under Islamic rule.	Christianity spreads throughout Anglo-Saxon world.
AD 750	Abbasid Caliphate established in Baghdad. Jerash begins its final decline.	Europe in the Dark Ages.

PART ONE

Jerash, the Decapolis and the Roman Province of Arabia – historical outline

Jerash is one of the best preserved provincial Roman cities in the world. To walk through its Roman streets, theatres, temples, plazas, baths and marketplaces is always an exhilarating experience, transporting us back into the wealthy, magnificent world of Roman provincial cities during the 1st, 2nd and 3rd centuries AD. To stroll through the remains of its fifteen Byzantine churches is to share the new sense of faith that enveloped the Christian Byzantine inhabitants of the city in the 4th, 5th and 6th centuries. To wander among the remains of Umayyad homes, mosques and pottery kilns is to relive the march of time, in the early 7th century, when Islam conquered Byzantium and the Middle East evolved from a Christian into a Muslim community.

Jerash is a powerful architectural legacy from the days of the Roman Empire's eastwards expansion, from the 1st century BC to the early 4th century AD. But it is much more than just a Roman city, for its ruins do not take us back only to a point of time nearly 2000 years ago. It is a stilled but stately record of over 1000 years of human activity, in an area that was often the meeting point, or battleground, of some of the world's great civilisations. The Egyptians, Assyrians, Babylonians, Greeks, Romans, Nabataeans, Byzantines, Persians, and Muslims all passed through this land, either moving on or staking their claim to the earth and the allegiance of its people. For over 1000 years, from the 2nd century BC to the 9th century AD, Jerash was a city whose fortunes ebbed and flowed in line with the tides of history.

The broad record of that history is etched forever into the stones of the city, but its more enigmatic details have to be prised out painstakingly from clues, hints and suggestions, deciphered from inscriptions, excavations and literary references. For the last 175 years, scholars, archaeologists, historians and travellers have pieced together the history of Jerash, the city the Greeks called Antioch on the Chrysorhoas, and which the Romans knew as Gerasa.

Its most important legacies are its intact city plan, and the excellent preservation of its buildings, most of which date from the grand days of the 2nd century AD. This was one of the greatest periods of perhaps the most awesome international empire ever to exist on the face of the earth, the Roman Empire. If its eastward expansion was among its crowning achievements, the cities of the eastern provinces were the jewels of the Greco–Roman East. At Jerash, we start to understand what it all meant, and to visualize how beautiful life must have been for the citizens of this wealthy, secure and satisfied city.

Jerash nestles in a broad valley on both sides of Wadi Jerash, the River Chrysorhoas of old, some forty kilometres north of the Jordanian capital of Amman. To the north and south of the city, travellers entering Jerash today pass through well watered, tree-lined hills. Driving through these lush hills, one starts to appreciate the abundant agricultural resources that helped the ancient inhabitants of the area grow rich, and build their monumental city.

Lying as it does at an altitude of some 550 metres above sea level, Jerash enjoys a mild climate that has always been one of its important attributes. In the Middle East's Roman period, starting in 64 BC, it also found itself strategically located at the junction of two key international trade routes that linked Rome and the Mediterranean basin with the legendary resources of Arabia, India, China and the East. When the *Pax Romana* brought peace and security, and linked the city to the Roman road and communication system that spanned half the globe, Jerash was set for a period of unprecedented growth and wealth. The story of that wealth and of provincial Roman urbanism has been passed down to us in the stones and monuments of Jerash.

10

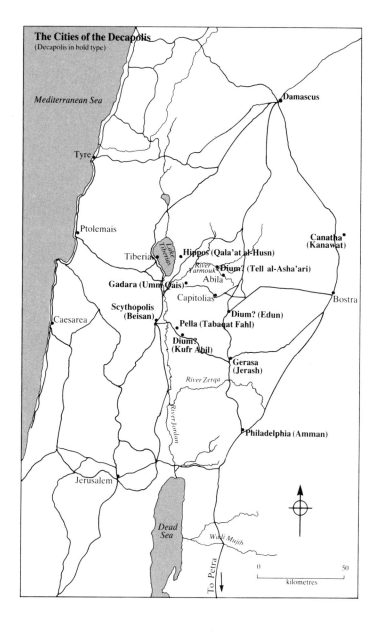

The Cities of the Decapolis
(Decapolis in bold type)

Mediterranean Sea

Damascus

Tyre

Ptolemais

Canatha
(Kanawat)

Tiberias
Lake Tiberias

Hippos (Qala'at al-Husn)

River Yarmouk

Dium? (Tell al-Asha'ari)

Abila

Gadara (Umm Qais)

Capitolias

Bostra

Scythopolis
(Beisan)

Dium? (Edun)

Pella (Tabaqat Fahl)

Caesarea

Dium?
(Kufr Abil)

Gerasa
(Jerash)

River Zerqa

River Jordan

Philadelphia (Amman)

Jerusalem

Dead
Sea

Wadi Mujib

To Petra

0   50
kilometres

THE DECAPOLIS

But Jerash was neither alone, nor unique. Its extensive, well preserved ruins, perhaps the most complete of any of the many Roman cities in the East, may give the false impression today that this was a singularly magnificent city in the midst of an otherwise mundane region. In fact, Jerash was one of dozens of similar provincial Roman cities throughout Syria and Arabia. For many decades, mainly during the first centuries BC and AD, it formed part of an association of ten Greco–Roman cities, known as the Decapolis, located throughout the area of modern Jordan, Syria and Palestine.

While ancient literary sources and maps clearly identify Jerash as a city of the Decapolis, the precise nature of the Decapolis itself is still vague. The word 'decapolis' is Greek for 'ten cities', though two Roman writers have left us slightly differing evidence of which cities formed the Decapolis.

Scholars of the nineteenth and early twentieth centuries viewed the Decapolis as a 'confederation' or 'league' of free Roman city-states, but this view has lost favour in recent years. The latest scholarship sees the Decapolis more as a region in northern Jordan and southern Syria where at least ten loosely associated provincial Roman cities and their territories flourished during the early centuries of Roman rule in the Middle East.

Many have assumed that the Decapolis came into existence in 63 BC, when Pompey conquered the area for Rome and included it in the Province of Syria. It probably ceased to exist in AD 106, when the Emperor Trajan annexed the Nabataean kingdom to the south and rearranged the Roman Empire's eastern flank by creating the new Roman Province of Arabia (*Provincia Arabia*). The former Decapolis cities were divided between the two provinces of Syria and Arabia, and ceased to enjoy their probably autonomous former status.

None of the historical references to the Decapolis from the 1st century AD onwards explains conclusively what the Decapolis was. It may well have been a formal league or confederation of politically allied Roman city-states, sharing common military, commercial and cultural interests, similar to other leagues of cities throughout the Roman provinces. It may only have been a convenient geographical designation for the region that included the ten cities. The Decapolis may have been a commercial unit, or simply an imperial administrative subdivision. It could also have had security considerations, acting as a buffer zone between the Roman Province of Syria to the north and the Nabataean Arab kingdom and adjacent desert regions to the south. It could have been all or several of these things at different times between the 1st century BC and the 2nd century AD, as the territory and political configuration of the Decapolis probably expanded, contracted and changed over time. The textual evidence provides many clues, but no conclusive proof.

The Decapolis is first mentioned in the biblical references in the books of Matthew and Mark, which say that Jesus passed through 'the region of the Decapolis' and crowds of people followed Jesus 'from Galilee and Decapolis and Jerusalem and Judaea and from the other side of the Jordan'. In both cases, the Decapolis seems to have a purely geographical meaning.

Josephus mentioned the Decapolis four times in his first-century AD works, referring to 'the inhabitants of the Decapolis', the 'chief men of the Syrian Decapolis', and 'the towns of the Syrian Decapolis'. He also says Scythopolis was the biggest of the Decapolis cities.

A recently reinterpreted inscription found in western Turkey a century ago recounts the career of a Roman equestrian officer. His service in the eastern provinces of the Roman Empire included a posting in 'the Decapolis of Syria', conclusively dated from the end of the 1st century AD. This inscription suggests the Decapolis was an administrative unit within the Province of Syria.

The Roman writer Pliny, in his *Natural History* completed in AD 77, says: 'Adjoining Judaea on the side of Syria is the region of the Decapolis, so called from the number of its towns, though not all writers keep to the same list . . .' He names the cities of the Decapolis as Damascus, Philadelphia, Raphana, Scythopolis, Gadara, Hippos, Dion, Pella, Galasa, and Canatha. ('Galasa' is a misspelling for Gerasa, or Jerash.)

In the 2nd century AD, the Egyptian–Roman geographer Ptolemy lists eighteen cities of Coele-Syria and the Decapolis in his *Geography*. Along with the ten Decapolis cities in Pliny's list, Ptolemy includes Abila, Capitolias, Heliopolis, Saana, Ina, Samoulis, Adra, and Abila Lysanios. Ptolemy seems to have combined two lists of cities of the Decapolis and of Coele-Syria.

Recent scholarship and excavation have identified the ten cities of the Decapolis as:

> Philadelphia (modern Amman)
> Gerasa (Jerash)
> Pella (Tabaqat Fahl)
> Scythopolis (Beisan, or Bethshean)
> Gadara (Umm Qais)
> Damascus
> Hippos (Qala'at al-Husn)
> Canatha (Kanawat, in southern Syria)
> Dium
> Raphana

The sites of ancient Dium and Raphana have not been conclusively identified. The four leading candidates for Dium are: Tell Husn and Edun, both near Irbid; Kufr Abil, near Pella; and Tell al-Asha'ari, near the Syrian border town of Dera'a.

It is noteworthy that not a single reference to the Decapolis comes from coins, inscriptions or other sources within the Decapolis region itself. Even though all the Decapolis cities minted their own coins, the word 'Decapolis' has never been found on any of their currency. The rather meagre evidence of the Decapolis and its recent interpretation by scholars does not support the old view of the Decapolis as a formal league or confederation of free or autonomous city–states established in 63 BC by Pompey. It may have been initially an administrative unit within the Province of Syria in the 1st century AD, grouping ten or more substantial provincial cities that shared a common Greco–Roman heritage and political interests. Though all the Decapolis cities except Damascus and Capitolias date their coins from their liberation by Pompey from the Hasmonaeans of Jerusalem in 63 BC, this probably reflects their gratitude to Pompey more than it signifies the start of a formal association among the cities at that time. After AD 106, however, the original significance of the term Decapolis was probably lost. But it remained in use until medieval times as a convenient name for the region of north Jordan and south Syria that once included the 'ten cities' in the early days of Rome's imperial conquests in the east.

One final point that should be made about the Decapolis

cities is that, sadly perhaps, they do not seem to have been a very conspicuous grouping within the context of the entire Roman Empire. The relatively few references to the Decapolis, in the otherwise rich material and textual remains from the Roman Empire, suggest this may have been a pleasant, prosperous but neglected corner of the Roman Empire, always in touch with the seat of power in Rome but never demanding much at all of its attention or resources. Once it was politically and militarily pacified in the 1st century BC, and secured permanently within a province of the Roman Empire, the region of the Decapolis flourished because of its abundant local resources and its strategic location astride the world's great east–west trade routes.

Its importance today reflects the substantial information some of its cities provide about the art and architecture of cities in the Roman Empire's eastern provinces. In this respect, Jerash is the most valuable of the Decapolis cities because so much of its Roman and Byzantine architecture is well preserved, within the neat order of its intact city plan.

The development of the area of modern Jordan in antiquity always reflected two dominant elements: the land's natural resources and location on the global trade routes; and its significance to more powerful political and military forces throughout the greater Middle East area. These two factors remain key determinants of Jordan's modern development, and therefore emphasise a recurring theme in the study of Jordanian history and archaeology; the growth or stagnation of the people of ancient Jordan has always been tightly bound with the physical and natural resources of the land, and its location within the broader context of the Middle East and Africa, Asia and Europe.

It is interesting that the ancient land of Jordan nurtured only one civilization that stands out in antiquity as worthy of international note: the Nabataean Arabs. From their base in southern Jordan and their secure capital city of Petra, the Nabataeans dominated the ancient world's trading pivot, at the junction of the trade routes connecting Europe, the Middle East, North Africa, South Asia and the Far East. Fortuitous historical circumstances allowed the Nabataeans to spread out from their southern Jordan heartland and control the whole territory of modern Jordan along with an area of the Middle East that stretched from southern Syria to the Sinai and Gaza, and to northern Arabia. But in their cultural glory and their rather widespread political control, the Nabataeans seem to be an exception to the rule of ancient Jordan. In all other periods of history, the civilisations of this land were generally of two types: narrowly defined, geographically constrained kingdoms that flourished within a small area (the Edomites, the Moabites and the Ammonites, for example), or less self-reliant local cultures that paid tribute to and intermingled with the more powerful forces that swirled around them throughout history: the Mesopotamian, Assyrian, Persian, Egyptian, Hellenistic, Roman, Byzantine and Islamic civilisations.

The earliest evidence of human activity at Jerash does not come from the area within the ancient city walls, but rather from the low hills surrounding the city. Mrs Diana Kirkbride-Helbaek carried out a survey of the area east and north of Jerash in the summer of 1955, and studied some pre-Roman sites that had been spotted previously by G. Lankester Harding and Nelson Glueck.

The most important pre-Roman site in the vicinity is Abu Suwan, which in Arabic means 'father of flint'. The site is on a long hill that slopes southwards to a point where Wadi Jerash meets another small wadi from the west, making for a good year-round supply of water. The site now lies within a farmer's field, located just east of the Amman–Jerash road, about 100 metres south-east of Hadrian's Arch.

Surface collections and a small trench dug by Mrs Kirkbride-Helbaek turned up a few late Stone Age handaxes from the Acheulian period and some Lavallois stone blades. Most of the artefacts, however, were flint implements from the Neolithic period (8000–4500 BC), and included barbed arrowheads, sickle blades, burins, drills, cores, flakes, scrapers, fragments of basalt grinding-querns, pestles and mortars, and a single obsidian blade. The trench also produced many burnt and unburnt animal bones, usually broken open for their marrow. Bone implements included several polished pins and a long curved tooth pierced at the top to allow it to be suspended at the end of a string or leather strap. Three hearths, but no evidence of permanent structures, suggest this may have been a Neolithic campsite used by ancient nomads who were drawn both to the water and to the area's animal and plant resources.

Three other sites within a two-kilometre radius to the north and east of Jerash produced surface flint instruments and some pottery that seem to date from the Chalcolithic period (4500–3200 BC). The remains of some house walls and a series of large cairns, or stone burial mounds, also suggest a Chalcolithic date. Along with the pottery of the Bronze and Iron Age subsequently excavated within the city walls, this earlier material indicates that the greater Jerash area was inhabited intermittently over a period of time that must now be measured in thousands of years.

For about 950 years, from the beginning of Hellenism in the Middle East to the end of the Romano–Byzantine era, the land of Jordan played a relatively minor role in the history of the Greco–Roman Middle East. This was neither Egypt nor Syria, neither Phoenicia nor Carthage. Throughout the Greco–Roman centuries, from Alexander the Great's occupation of Syria in 332 BC to Constantine the Great's founding of Constantinople and the Byzantine Empire in AD 324, the region of Jordan and the Decapolis cities rose and fell in line with the tides of regional history. But that history was always made elsewhere, in imperial capitals such as Athens and Rome, or provincial capitals such as Antioch, Alexandria, Damascus or Bostra. The importance Rome attached to the lands of ancient Syria and Arabia reflected their value as producers of agricultural and industrial goods, and their strategic location astride the trade routes.

The Roman provinces of Syria, Arabia and Palestine, which at various times included the area of modern Jordan, always formed the south-eastern frontier of the Roman Empire. These were distant, strange, rough and rowdy lands peopled by Semitic tribes who had mastered the camel and tamed the desert, and boasted an urban tradition that was already thousands of years old when Greece and Rome stepped onto the Middle Eastern stage, flushed with imperial pride.

Throughout most of the nine and a half centuries from Greek to Byzantine rule in the Middle East, Jordan was either a vital link in the great east–west land route that carried the commerce of the ancient world, or it was a strategic frontier zone that warded off Rome's traditional enemies in the south-eastern corner of the empire: the Parthian and Sassanid civilisations to the east, and the troublesome, Saracen Arab tribes to the south.

The Greco–Roman influence in the Middle East was most visible in the development of cities, and it is in the remains of those cities that we can see today the most splendid achievements of Roman Arabia. But the tradition of urbanism, or village and city life, in the Middle East is measured in thousands of years. It was initially conceived in the Natufian villages of around 10,000 BC, passed through the Neolithic and Chalcolithic villages of the 9th–5th millennia BC, and entered a true 'city-state' concept with the walled towns of the Early Bronze Age, starting around 3200 BC. The Iron Age kingdoms of the Edomites, Ammonites and Moabites were dotted with walled towns whose massive, silent remains are scattered throughout Jordan.

During the Persian period, in the middle of the 1st millennium BC, a series of important cities flourished in two main strings of towns that ran in a north-south direction. The coastal cities along the Mediterranean were important sea ports, paralleled by another string of inland 'desert ports' that connected the coastal economies and cultures with the eastern deserts and the main trade route to Arabia and the east. While the basis for life in the Persian Middle East was predominantly village-based agriculture under the aegis of great tribal associations, the cities of the coast and the inland trade routes completed the infrastructure that was the essential basis of security and the rich trade that went with it. Some of the older coastal cities included Gaza, Ascalon, Acre, Tyre, Sidon and Byblos. The string of inland commercial cities that traded with their coastal counterparts included Damascus, Hama, Aleppo, and, further south in the land of Jordan, probably smaller urban centres such as Rabbath Ammon (Amman), Pella, Heshbon (Hisban), Madaba, Kerak and Petra. Some of these cities were small units that may have flourished and expanded during the Persian period, when the link between tribal and political power would have been strong, particularly in the inland cities.

THE HELLENISTIC ERA

When Alexander the Great occupied Syria in 332 BC, he found a land with a handful of important trade-oriented cities and towns, surrounded by a wide area of tribal and village-based agriculture and pastoral nomadism. The entire structure of life was loosely watched over by the governors and representatives of the Persian Empire, whose main interest was probably collecting tributes and making sure that peace reigned in the land.

The advent of Hellenism in the Middle East profoundly influenced the development of cities from the middle of the 4th century BC. The vehicle for the spread of Hellenistic influence in the area was initially the planting of garrisons of Macedonian settler–soldiers, first under Alexander himself, and later under his successors, notably Perdiccas. Many of the cites that claimed to have been 'founded' by Alexander already had long urban histories; in some cases, such as Amman, Pella, and Scythopolis, these cities dated back many thousands of years.

The initial Macedonian settlements gradually developed into towns and fully fledged cities during the century after the death of Alexander, when his successors continually fought each other for control of the Hellenistic lands of the Middle East. Ptolemy took Egypt, while Seleucus took Babylonia and northern Syria, having defeated Antigonus in 301 BC and firmly secured the eastern lands of the Hellenistic Middle East. The region of the Decapolis cities, in north Jordan and south Syria, remained hotly contested for over a century between the Ptolemies and the Seleucids. For most of the 3rd century BC, the Ptolemies controlled Palestine and the Phoenician coast, while the Seleucids ruled in north Syria, with the precise demarcation of their areas of control shifting occasionally. Only after the Seleucid King Antiochus III defeated the Ptolemies at the Battle of Panium in 200 BC and signed a treaty with them did the entire area of Syria, Jordan and Palestine finally and officially become part of the Seleucid Empire.

During the 3rd century BC, Hellenistic settlements populated by Macedonians and Athenians were established throughout the Middle East, and slowly grew into flourishing towns. The cities of the Decapolis trace their Greco–Roman origins back to this period, with some of the cities, such as Philadelphia (Amman), being Ptolemaic colonies, others Seleucid. The Seleucids were far more active than the Ptolemies in settling the area of Jordan–Syria, as this was the heartland of their empire, while the Ptolemies were busier settling Egypt.

The precise nature of the early Hellenistic colonies remains unclear. In some cases, entirely new cities were founded by

Macedonian settlers. In other cases, existing cities were expanded and renamed. The degree of independence exercised by the cities, and the territories they controlled, also remain vague. The political structure and administrative and judicial organisation of the young Hellenistic cities reflected a totally Greek concept of democratic municipal life, in which the people held ultimate power and administered public affairs through elected officials and an appointed civil service. The introduction of the Greek language into the area initially affected only an urban elite, who had to use Greek for official business. Most of the countryside continued to use the local language, Aramaic.

The earliest days of Jerash remain clouded in the haze of Middle Eastern Hellenism. The Greco–Roman name of the city, Gerasa, was the Hellenised version of its Semitic name, 'Garshu'. This is confirmed by a Nabataean inscription found on a small carved obelisk at Petra, one of the many commemorative funerary obelisks found throughout the Nabataean capital city. The inscription remembered a certain citizen of Petra named Petraios, son of Threptos, who died at Garshu and was buried there.

A 2nd-century AD inscription found near the Temple of Artemis refers to the city as 'Antioch on the Chrysorhoas also called Gerasa'. Other Roman inscriptions refer to Jerash as 'the city of the Antiochenes on the Chrysorhoas, formerly of the Gerasenes'. The Chrysorhoas ('Golden River') was the name of the stream that flowed through the centre of the city.

Archaeological, historical and inscriptional evidence studied to date suggests that the first proper walled Hellenistic 'city' was established on the present site sometime during the 2nd century BC. This is the period from which we have the earliest historical reference to the city. The Roman historian Josephus mentions that Theodorus and Zeno, the 'tyrants' of Philadelphia, brought some of their treasure for safekeeping to the Temple of Zeus at Jerash. The recent French excavations of the foundation walls of the Temple of Zeus *temenos* uncovered stone floor levels from the middle of the 2nd century BC.

Most evidence supports the theory that a small Hellenistic, or even pre-Hellenistic, settlement was turned into a Hellenistic *polis*, or city, after the Seleucid King Antiochus III (223–187 BC) controlled the area, following the Battle of Panium in 200 BC. Other theories have it that his son, Antiochus IV, 'founded' the city, or that it was founded by Alexander the Great himself or his successors Perdiccas or Antigonus in the late 4th century or 3rd century BC. At whatever date the city of Jerash was formally founded, it was clearly an established urban centre by the early 2nd century BC.

By the middle of the 2nd century BC, opposition to Hellenism in Judaea was growing, while both the Ptolemaic and Seleucid empires were starting to show signs of internal weakness and disintegration. Judas Maccabeus rose to power in Judaea following a revolt against the Seleucids in 173–164 BC, and took control of all the Decapolis cities except for Damascus, Philadelphia and Canatha. He was defeated soon after by the Seleucids in the Battle of Elasa, but the civil wars and disintegration of the Seleucid Empire had started in earnest. The new Hasmonaean dynasty of Judaea would soon launch another campaign to control the lands east of the Jordan. This came in 103 BC, when Alexander Jannaeus took power in Judaea, and attacked and occupied the Hellenistic cities east of the Jordan, including Abila, Hippos, Pella, Gadara, Dium and Madaba. Philadelphia and Gerasa remained in the hands of a local tyrant king, Zeno Cotylas, and his son Theodorus. All the Decapolis cities except for Damascus fell under Hasmonaean influence.

While the Judaean house in Palestine was asserting itself at the expense of the Seleucids, so were two other local tribal powers: the Nabataean Arabs in southern Jordan and northern Arabia, and the Ituraeans in east Lebanon and north-eastern Palestine. The Ituraeans expanded their control in the north and virtually encircled the important Seleucid city of Damascus. They would have taken it, had not the Seleucids called on the Nabataeans for help. The Nabataean King Aretas III responded, and thereafter ruled the great city of Syria for fifteen years. War had also broken out several times between the Nabataeans and the Hasmonaeans of Judaea in the early days of the 1st century BC.

Thus, in the first half of the 1st century BC, the greater region within which the Decapolis cities were located was in considerable turmoil. The break-up of the former Seleucid Empire ushered in a period during which the area was constantly contested among major local powers such as the Nabataeans, the Ituraeans and the Hasmonaeans. The anarchy was exacerbated after the death of the Judaean ruler Alexander Jannaeus, when three Judaean tribes fought each other for control of the former Hasmonaean kingdom. Local tribal and 'bandit' chieftains, princelings, city governors and other small-time tyrants and pretenders to power asserted their control wherever they could, while the invading forces of the Armenian kingdom to the north were also a constant threat. This disarray and lawlessness finally pushed the security-conscious Romans of the north to take matters into their own hands. Rome was also keen to preempt a potentially threatening Parthian move westwards through the disintegrating Seleucid Empire towards the Mediterranean.

THE ROMAN ERA

In 65–64 BC, the forces of the Roman General Pompey marched southwards and took Damascus. Rome had to establish the defence of the territories further south if its interests in Syria were to be secure, and this caused Pompey to become involved in the affairs of both the Nabataeans of Arabia and the Jews of Judaea. In 64 BC Pompey himself arrived in Damascus, and made the major political decision that would usher in the long era of Roman rule in the land of the Decapolis cities, and in the broader regions of Syria and Arabia. After repulsing the Armenian King Tigranes and annexing the Seleucid capital of Antioch, Pompey created the Roman Province of Syria.

A key element in Pompey's reorganization of the east was his emphasis on the important role of the former Greek city–states. These served both to spread Greco–Roman culture, and to act as a counterforce to the power of local Semitic tribes and kingdoms on the frontier of the Empire. The cities of the Decapolis were an important part of Pompey's mission. They were 'freed' by Pompey and given back their autonomy, but they remained under the overall aegis of the Province of Syria to the north.

The Judaean Kingdom was subdued in 63 BC when Pompey took Jerusalem and gave Rome's backing to Hyrcanus. The Nabataeans had largely withdrawn into their secure heartland in southern Jordan. Thus, by 63 BC Pompey had fully reorganised and secured the lands of Syria, Palestine and northern Arabia that had been in such turmoil for the previous 150 years. Pompey returned to Rome in 62 BC, leaving behind Aemilius Scaurus to run the Province of Syria. He secured his southern frontier in 62 BC when the Nabataeans paid tribute to him and thereby warded off a threatened Roman invasion of Nabataea. The final pacification of the area came in 38 BC, when the Romans repulsed the Parthians to the east and launched the Province of Syria into centuries of peace, prosperity and development. The lands and peoples of northern Arabia, Syria, Palestine and Jordan were either firmly under Roman rule, or practised a good-neighbour policy that allowed them to flourish under the broad security and prosperity that came with the *Pax Romana*, or 'Roman peace'.

The new era of peace once again allowed the cities of the Decapolis to play their previous role as the purveyors of Greco–Roman culture, though the surrounding countryside maintained its solid, local Semitic culture, language and religion. Trade remained the primary source of their wealth, and was supplemented by local industry and agriculture.

By the early years of the 1st century AD, Judaea was formally annexed into the Roman Empire, and the Emperor Augustus was eyeing the formidable wealth of the Sabaean Arabs in the area of modern Yemen, in the south-western corner of the Arabian Peninsula. The Nabataean Arabs continued to flourish in southern Jordan and northern Arabia, reaching the peak of their brilliant architectural achievements in the rock-cut monuments of Petra, and at Medain Saleh in northern Saudi Arabia. Their prosperity was also based on a combination of trade and agriculture, as they gradually dropped their nomadic lifestyle and settled into an increasingly urban mode of life.

The second important reorganisation of the Roman east came in AD 106, when the expansionist Emperor Trajan annexed the Nabataean kingdom. He created the new Roman Province of Arabia (*Provincia Arabia*), and the cities of the Decapolis were distributed between the provinces of Arabia and Syria: Gerasa, Philadelphia, Dium, and Canatha became part of the Province of Arabia, while the others joined the Province of Syria. The capital of the Province of Arabia was at Bostra, in southern Syria, and the former Decapolis cities in Arabia were under the political and military control of the Roman provincial governor based there. Gerasa suddenly found itself in the heart of the new Province, well situated to take advantage of the economic benefits that came with its strategic location.

The cities of the Decapolis prospered handsomely under the new arrangement, continuing to play their previous roles as entrepôts and caravan cities along a major international trade route. The skeleton around which the body of the new Province of Arabia prospered was the network of paved, secure roads built during Trajan's reign. Its backbone was the *Via Nova Traiana*, or Trajan's New Road, built under the aegis of Claudius Severus, the first governor of the new Arabian province. Something of a superhighway for its time, it stretched for nearly 500 kilometres, linking the Roman port of Aila (Aqaba) with the provincial capital at Bostra. It has been dubbed by some scholars 'the greatest piece of Roman road-making in the Orient'.

The *Via Nova* was both an important trade artery and a vital military road, allowing either Roman troops or traders to travel swiftly along its route in total comfort and security. It was also a key segment of the southernmost east–west trade route that linked Rome and the Mediterranean world with southern Arabia, India, China and the east.

Jerash was slightly off the path of the *Via Nova*, which went in a north-easterly direction from Philadelphia (Amman) on an almost straight line to Bostra. Several branch roads connected Jerash with other Decapolis cities, such as Philadelphia, Dium, Bostra and Pella, thereby firmly linking it and its rich agricultural territory into the network of trade and prosperity that grew up around the *Via Nova* and within the *Pax Romana*. A key link was the north-western road that left Jerash's North Gate and travelled to Pella, in the Jordan Valley. From there it crossed the River Jordan to Scythopolis (Beisan), and continued westwards to the Mediterranean coastal cities of Caesarea and Ptolemais.

Trade from the Orient moving westwards passed through the Arabian peninsula to the cities in the land of Jordan that served as collection and distribution points. From here, it either moved westwards to the port-emporiums of Gaza and Alexandria, or northwards on the *Via Nova*. At Philadelphia, goods moved either on the north-eastern road to Bostra, Damascus and Antioch, or on the north-western road to Jerash, Pella, Scythopolis, Caesarea and Ptolemais.

By the end of the reign of the Emperor Hadrian (AD 117–

138), the Roman road network in Jordan–Palestine was complete. It consisted of at least two main north–south arteries: the inland *Via Nova*, linking the Red Sea with Bostra, Damascus and Antioch; and the Mediterranean coastal highway that linked Alexandria in Egypt with the Palestinian and Phoenician cities, going northwards all the way to Antioch. A further north–south road is known to have been built by Diocletian, though its exact route is not known. Not only did Jerash lie close to the *Via Nova*, but it was also a key junction along the road that connected Philadelphia with the Mediterranean cities, one of the most important east–west land links between the two major Roman road systems of the day.

Bostra flourished because it was strategically situated at the point of convergence of the two main overland trade routes from Arabia: the *Via Nova* from Aqaba and the western coast of the Arabian peninsula, and the more easterly desert route that started along the Gulf shore of eastern Arabia, passing north-west through Wadi Sirhan into north Jordan and finally to Bostra.

The annexation of Nabataea and the expansion of the Roman Empire further south in AD 106 appear to have been accomplished peacefully. The annexation brought with it a presence of Roman troops throughout the new province. One of their first and most important activities was to start building the impressive network of Roman roads that criss-crossed the province and made it such an important transit route for international trade for the next several hundred years.

The two most important cities of the Province of Arabia were Bostra and Petra. The high volume of traffic and trade between them, given the security provided by the area's formal inclusion in the Roman Empire, guaranteed a considerable source of wealth. The caravan cities on the route north to Bostra and Antioch entered a period of development in the 1st and 2nd centuries AD that was sustained for several hundred years. The legacy of that period of impressive urban development includes the surviving ruins of cities such as Gerasa, Philadelphia, Petra and Palmyra.

During its initial growth years in the 1st century AD, Jerash must have had strong commercial links with the Nabataean capital of Petra to the south, in keeping with the political *modus vivendi* that had been worked out between the Roman and Nabataean powers in the area. Nabataean inscriptions and coins found at Jerash provide only tantalizing clues about the nature of ties between Jerash and Petra, and the cultural influence that the Nabataeans must have exerted on their Gerasene contemporaries to the north.

An important bilingual Greco–Nabataean inscription found on the slope of Camp Hill in 1931 refers to a statue erected in honour of two Nabataean kings. The first named is Aretas, most probably King Aretas IV (9 BC–AD 40). The text also includes the phrase '. . . for the life of our lord Rabbel, king . . .', suggesting the statue was meant to honour both an Aretas and a Rabbel. The most likely Rabbel was the grandson of Aretas IV, the Nabataean King Rabbel II (AD 70–106), during whose reign the statue may have been erected.

Professor Kraeling says that it 'is tempting to infer from the wording of the text that the Nabataean community had special rights and privileges at Gerasa, as the citizens of Palmyra seem to have had at Dura. Perhaps it was incorporated as a separate *ethnos* in the organization of the city'. Mr C. B. Welles, who published the Jerash inscriptions from the 1920s and 30s, wonders whether the inscription's compass references 'west' and 'south' may designate a piece of land, perhaps near the city walls, that had been donated by a Nabataean merchant at Gerasa, 'to provide income for the service of a god, in connection with which he erected a statue and an inscription invoking blessings on the ruling family of his homeland'.

Other inscriptions found mainly in the area around the Cathedral, and dating from the late 1st century AD and mid-2nd century AD, speak of the Nabataean 'holy god' Pakidas, and his consort Hera, and of the mysterious 'Arabian god'. Kraeling and Crowfoot suggest the existing Cathedral may have been built on the site of the Roman temple dedicated to Dionysus. The Roman god Dionysus, in turn, is often identified with the Nabataean god Dusares, and a 1st-century AD Ionic temple dedicated to the god Dusares–Dionysus stood for many years on the spot of the present Cathedral. The Gerasene 'Arabian god', known to us only from inscription fragments of the 1st and 2nd century AD, may well have been none other than the important deity Dusares–Dionysus, though only further inscriptional evidence can verify or refute this possible association.

The flourishing of Gerasa and other former Decapolis cities in the 2nd and 3rd centuries AD was not a sudden occurrence. Rather, as we have seen, the urban tradition of the region already dated back thousands of years. The city of Gerasa, in its existing form, started as a Hellenistic entity, but little of the Greek city has ever been found or excavated. A small, walled Hellenistic city would have been located probably in the area on and around Camp Hill, overlooking the Oval Plaza from the east. Excavations and inscriptions show that Gerasa started to spread in the 1st century BC soon after Pompey 'freed' it in 63 BC. Major building activity started in earnest in the first half of the 1st century AD, both in the south, near Camp Hill and the Temple of Zeus, and in the north near the first Temple of Artemis.

View of the Cardo, looking towards the North Tetrapylon (*drawn by Warwick Ball*) (see p. 67)

· The existing ruins in Jerash and the overall town plan date mainly from the 2nd century AD, reflecting the building spree that followed Trajan's annexation of Nabataea and the establishment of the Province of Arabia. The basis for the 2nd-century urban development, however, can be traced back to around AD 50–75. This was when the basic town plan of Gerasa was formulated, key elements of which were the intersecting main streets of the city and its outer walls. In the following centuries, individual monuments and even entire neighbourhoods or public areas of the city would be built and rebuilt. But the growth and occasional redevelopment of the city would always fit into the general plan established in the middle of the 1st century. This plan revolved around the colonnaded main street, the Cardo, and the two intersecting colonnaded side streets, the North and South Decumanus. The city walls and gates were first built towards the end of the 1st century AD. Some of the city's most important public monuments, thoroughfares and open spaces were established at this time, including the South Theatre, the Oval Plaza and the Cardo.

The prosperity that came with the Trajianic era (AD 98–117) continued during the reign of the Emperor Hadrian (AD 117–138). Hadrian himself travelled through the Province of Arabia in AD 129/130, and spent some time at Gerasa. The city marked this high honour by building a richly decorated triumphal arch, known today as Hadrian's Arch. It is the first monument one sees when approaching Jerash from the south, and it stands rather alone because the original plans to expand the city walls to meet up with it were never implemented.

The middle of the 2nd century AD was a prosperous, stable era for Gerasa, as we can discern from the burst of elaborate, monumental, and no doubt expensive construction in all quarters of the city. The glorious development of the city continued through the Antonine years, in the second half of the 2nd century AD. Jerash reflects the 'Golden Age', during which a new Temple of Artemis complex was constructed and dedicated around AD 150. The majestic new temple within its enormous *temenos*, or sacred precinct, effectively shifted the focus of the city north from its former centre around the Oval Plaza and the Temple of Zeus. Open spaces, such as plazas, streets and intersections, became a more important architectural feature in Gerasa, as they did in many other cities throughout the eastern Roman provinces that were strongly influenced by a Syrian or Eastern school of architecture. Streets and plazas that had been used as a method of dividing parts of the older Greek and early Roman city became more autonomous architectural spaces in the 2nd century. Open spaces, such as the Oval Plaza, took on their own form and provided aesthetic interest for the citizens of the city, who spent so much of their time walking around Gerasa. Large sidewalks throughout the city were a relatively new development, and a citizen of 2nd-century Gerasa walking in any part of the city would have found aesthetically pleasing architectural vistas all around him. No longer did Gerasa have one focal point in the southern area around the Temple of Zeus. Rather, the wealthy, dynamic city built a whole new series of important civic monuments, including the Artemis Temple complex, the North Theatre complex, the widened Cardo with new Corinthian capitals, the Nymphaeum, the South Tetrakionion and a new Temple of Zeus complex.

Transit trade, local agriculture and some small-scale industry provided the city's wealth, which was generated and assured by the political security that came with being a part of the Roman Empire. The *Pax Romana*, or 'Roman peace', combined with the international road and shipping network established by the Romans, opened up enormous new markets in the west that would be quickly exploited by the legendary merchants of Syria. Their business centred around major Syrian cities such as Antioch, Damascus and Bostra. Relative to them, Jerash was well situated to take advantage of the transit traffic that passed through it, on its way from the east to the heartland of the Empire in Rome, Europe and the Mediterranean basin.

The city derived much of its income from the taxes it levied on passing caravans. Commercial records from Jerash are scarce, but it would have had a similar tariff structure to that of Palmyra, which has been preserved. Taxes were levied on specific items, such as 25 denarii for each camel-load of myrrh imported in alabaster vessels, 13 denarii for each camel-load of olive oil imported in four goatskins, 3 denarii for each camel-load of dried products, 2 denarii for each donkey-load of dry products, and 22 denarii for each imported slave.

For over 150 years, a prosperous Jerash provided its citizens with the security, amenities and pleasures that were part of the good life throughout the provincial cities of the Roman east. If the city has left us a powerful testament to its glory in the form of its many splendid monuments, far less is known about the precise nature of political, social and economic life during its years of splendour in the 1st to 3rd centuries AD.

Few residential quarters of the city have been excavated, making it difficult to estimate the size of the population. Certainly, there were substantial areas within the city walls that were never built up, particularly in the northern and western quarters. The residential quarter of the city must have been located on the east bank of the river, underneath the modern city of Jerash, though the remains of some houses have been uncovered on the west bank, west and north-west of the Oval Plaza. The city's population at its height may have reached 20–25,000 people in the 2nd century AD, with thousands more living in villages and farmsteads in the surrounding area.

Agriculture was an important element in the city's wealth. Many of the rich Gerasenes were probably large absentee landowners who lived in the city. They would also have maintained country villas, and appointed farm managers to run their estates. Most of the agricultural produce was locally consumed, or traded within the territory controlled by the city.

The Decapolis cities, like provincial Roman cities throughout the Empire, administered the lands and people in their immediate vicinity. It is likely that the territories of the separate Decapolis cities bordered on one another, forming a contiguous region that promoted security, economic and social ties among the people of the Decapolis. The precise territory that Jerash controlled is not known, though it must have been substantial to provide the obvious wealth that the city enjoyed. Scholars who have tried to determine the territories of Decapolis cities, by studying the milestones along the Roman roads, suggest Gerasa's territory formed a rough square about 25 kilometres north to south and 30 kilometres east to west. Its southern border generally followed the line of the Zerqa river. Its eastern border was just before the town of Rihab. To the north, it bordered on the territory of Pella, and to the west on the territory of Peraea. To the east was the territory of Bostra, and to the south lay Philadelphia.

Ethnically, the citizens of Jerash were predominantly of local Semitic stock, with an overlay of Greco–Romans who first came to the region as officials or soldiers. In the 1st and 2nd centuries AD, only a small minority of the population would have been full Roman citizens, paying special taxes and enjoying equally special privileges. Locally recruited soldiers, or auxillaries, became Roman citizens upon their discharge from the army after twenty-five years of service, when they would normally have been granted a plot of land and a cash payment. In AD 211, the Emperor Caracalla decreed that all residents of Roman provincial cities were to become full citizens, thereby blurring the political and social distinctions that had prevailed among the inhabitants of the eastern provinces.

The citizens of Jerash used a variety of languages simultaneously. The Semitic population, especially in the countryside, spoke the local dialect of Aramaic, while within the city Greek and Latin were more common. Latin was the formal language of the Empire, used in official documents and correspondence, while Greek was the more commonly spoken language. Of the several hundred inscriptions found at Jerash, the vast majority are in Greek, with only some fifteen per cent in Latin. Similarly, inscriptions giving the names of the prominent citizens of Jerash who donated money to finance public monuments reveal that the majority were Greek, with only a few Semitic or Latin names.

This blend of eastern and Greco–Roman languages was typical of the ethnic and cultural mix of people and traditions throughout the cities of the eastern Roman provinces. Jerash was not an isolated island of pure Greco–Roman culture planted in the midst of a hostile and alien Middle-Eastern, Semitic environment. This was, at its core, a Semitic society, but one which had absorbed a thick veneer of Greco–Roman language, ideas, names and political structures. Jerash reflected, and was itself, a synthesis of eastern and Greco–Roman ideas and styles, also evident in such fields as religion and architecture.

In a recent analysis of architectural representations on coins from several Decapolis cities, Julian Bowsher suggests that the Roman temples of the Decapolis reveal 'an older cultural heritage'. Some eastern, or Syrian, cultic traditions were incorporated into Roman temple designs, including siting temples on heights, or 'High Places', and placing temples within a sacred area, or *temenos*. In both cases, the temples of Zeus and Artemis at Jerash reflect these ancient local traditions.

The gods that were worshipped within the temples of the Decapolis cities may also derive from divinities that had been worshipped by the indigenous population for thousands of years.

The Semitic deity most often associated with high places was Baal Shamin, who was subsequently associated with Zeus during the Greco–Roman era. It has been suggested that many of the gods worshipped in the Decapolis, such as Helios, Artemis, Zeus and Tyche, emerged from centuries of blending among Semitic and Greco–Roman deities, with many of the eastern gods originating perhaps in the mythology of the Phoenicians.

If the Decapolis cities were linked with Phoenicia by religion, they also certainly had strong commercial ties with the Phoenician cities along the Mediterranean coast of modern Lebanon. An inscription from Jerash tells of a Marcus Aurelius Maro, who lived in the early days of the 3rd century AD. He enjoyed the title of 'Phoenicarch', whose precise meaning remains unknown to modern historians. This is thought to be an honourary title related to an imperial cult that held great provincial festivals in honour of the emperors. A city counsellor and a priest, Maro was most likely a wealthy Gerasene who had strong trading links with such Phoenician cities as Tyre, Sidon and Ptolemais. Trade between Jerash and the Mediterranean coastal cites was an important source of income for the city. It travelled via a network of good Roman roads that passed from Jerash's North Gate, to Pella and Scythopolis (Beisan) in the Jordan Valley, to Caesarea and Ptolemais on the Palestine coast, and from there northwards to the great Phoenician trading and sea-faring cities.

Marcus Aurelius Maro may have been typical of the wealthy merchants who dominated the city's commercial and political life during its golden years. Numerous inscriptions, discovered and studied by the team of Anglo–American scholars in the 1920s and 1930s, record the generosity of wealthy Gerasenes who donated money to build or maintain public monuments. Religious buildings were a special focus of their philanthropy.

Throughout the second half of the 1st century AD, for example, while work was progressing on the South Theatre, the Temple of Zeus and the Temple of Artemis, numerous citizens donated money to help finance these projects, and carefully recorded their munificence in stone for future generations to remember. A certain Theon, son of Demetrius, seems to have donated substantially towards the construction of the Temple of Zeus and its propylaeum. Another wealthy donor was Titus

Flavius, son of Dionysius, who paid for a block of seats in the South Theatre. To the north, a certain Diogenes, son of Leonidas, dedicated an altar he had financed for the Temple of Artemis in AD 98. Similar acts of public generosity were repeated throughout the city, both by groups such as the guilds of potters, linen weavers and retail traders, and by satisfied, civic-minded merchants and leading families who no doubt felt obliged to mark their gratitude for the opportunity the city of Jerash had given them to rise to stations of prosperity and public esteem.

Inscriptional evidence of public officials' titles has left us a clearer picture of the city's political and administrative organisation. The citizens and businessmen of Jerash paid a series of taxes that included a head tax on individuals, property taxes and commercial taxes, paid either to the local city treasury or to the imperial treasury that was represented by the governor at the provincial capital at Bostra. The provincial governor was the region's top judicial and military official, and he or his representatives made regular trips to other provincial cities to deal with the sort of issues that have occupied the time and minds of regional officials from the earliest days of recorded history – road systems, military service, the civil service and the promotion of officials, trade, financing public buildings and the like. Some of the provincial taxes were sent back to the seat of the Empire in Rome, while the balance financed local projects, such as roads, water works and endeavours related to security.

The Jerash city government would have included a people's assembly grouping all the residents of the city. This was largely a relic from the Hellenistic concept of 'government by the people', and had little real power. The city council, or *boule*, was typically composed of fifty representatives from each of the ten or twelve local tribes. The city council met regularly and wielded real legislative authority, though it usually took its cue from the true power centre of the city, the *archons*, or city magistrates, who were elected annually by the city council.

The *archons* were, effectively, the city government cabinet, composed of a handful of five or six magistrates headed by a *proedos*, or president, and including a secretary. Other magistrates were responsible for specific areas of city life, such as games and recreation, public works, or finances. To be elected as a magistrate, an individual normally had to achieve a certain level of personal wealth. The elected magistrates were usually rotated to maintain an equitable balance of representation among the city's tribes, families and professions.

When the political situation in Rome itself started to deteriorate in the second half of the 2nd century AD, the ripples of instability took a very long time to reach the Province of Arabia and its flourishing cities in the south-eastern corner of the Empire. Jerash and the other cities of the Decapolis were fortunate to find themselves at the heart of an international commercial network during what some historians have called 'the greatest economic boom the ancient world was ever to know'. Jerash and its sister cities in the provinces of Syria and Arabia thought they could only grow, and become richer and more beautiful. Until the end of the 2nd century AD, they did.

By the early years of the 3rd century, however, the picture started to change. The troubles in Rome finally caught up with the provincial cities, as political instability and economic vulnerabilities loosened the cohesion of the Empire. In the early part of the 3rd century, the Emperor Caracalla (AD 211–217) raised the status of Gerasa to that of a colony, called Colonia Aurelia Antoniniana, but this did not appear to change the city's fading fortunes. A series of successive emperors of widely different capabilities ruled briefly over an Empire increasingly troubled by civil war and economic problems during most of the 3rd century AD.

To make things worse, Rome's internal turmoil made it more vulnerable to old enemies along its frontiers. The Sassanids in Persia were the most dangerous threat to the Empire from the east. Several times they invaded Roman Syria and captured the great city of Antioch, and in AD 260 they defeated a Roman army of some 70,000 and took prisoner the Emperor Valerian.

During the 2nd century, the Nabataeans in south Jordan had started to relinquish their political and economic power, and a new Arab power rose in the form of the desert kingdom of Palmyra. The commercially minded Palmyrenes, relying as they did on secure, long-range trade routes, were also a military power. They came to the aid of Rome after the capture of Antioch in AD 260 and repulsed the Sassanid invasion, carving out for themselves a special role as the protectors of Roman frontier interests in the east.

With regional and international trade badly hampered by political instability, the basis of Jerash's prosperity started to disappear during the 3rd century. Gone were the years of widespread, lavish construction of monumental civic complexes. In the 3rd century, major new construction projects at Jerash included only the East Baths, the Festival Theatre at Birketein, and the expansion of the North Theatre.

By the end of the 3rd century, the Emperor Diocletian had halted briefly the decline of Roman Syria and Arabia. He reorganised internal political affairs, enlarged the imperial army and tried to reform the economic system of the Empire by revising taxation, issuing new currency and imposing strict but ineffective price and wage controls. He also undertook a substantial rearrangement of the provinces. It was during his reign that the existing city walls of Jerash were built.

After the Sassanid threat was finally dealt with in the east, he rearranged the administrative borders of the provinces of Syria and Arabia. The southern part of Palestine, including Jordanian territory south of Wadi Hasa, was eventually transformed into *Palestina Tertia*. Trade flowed across this area, predominantly in an east–west direction, linking Aila (Aqaba) with Petra, Wadi Araba, the Naqab (Negev), Gaza, the Sinai, Egypt and the Mediterranean. Security for south Jordan was provided by an increased presence of Roman troops, at the legionary camps of Lejjun and Udruh, both of which can be visited today.

The remainder of the Province of Arabia in the north was also reorganised and strengthened militarily. Wadi Sirhan, the old route from eastern Arabia to Bostra and Damascus, re-emerged as an important trade route, thanks to the security that Diocletian's rule brought to the area. Relative prosperity would follow for Jerash and the other trading cities in the region of the Decapolis.

While Jerash and the other leading Roman cities in Jordan never regained their former wealth or beauty, they did enjoy a brief period of stability and development during the Diocletian years. But it was something of a swansong, for the city's fortunes declined steadily from that point on, and never again would Jerash attain its former glory or wealth.

THE BYZANTINE ERA

Diocletian had divided the Roman Empire into eastern and western halves. By AD 286, he ruled the eastern provinces from his new court at Nicomedia, near the Black Sea. In the meantime, the relatively new religion of Christianity was gaining ground throughout the Empire. Relations between Christians and the Roman state became a key political issue in the early 4th century and by the time of Diocletian's abdication and the arrival of the Emperor Constantine in AD 312, the well organised Christians were thought to account for about ten per cent of the population of the Empire.

Constantine the Great established the new capital of the Eastern Roman Empire at Byzantium, site of the former Greek colony, which was strategically located to oversee the defence of the two important frontier zones along the Danube and the Euphrates. The new capital of Constantinople, or New Rome, on the site of present-day Istanbul, was formally dedicated on 11 May, 330.

The establishment of Constantinople had come during a period of two decades when Christianity was gaining both a greater popular following throughout the Empire and increasing official tolerance. A series of edicts as of AD 313 had granted Christians the right to practise their religion. By 324, Christianity had been officially proclaimed the religion of the Empire, and Constantinople was established as an emphatically Christian capital city.

As had happened throughout the centuries of the Roman Empire, political, economic and cultural stimuli from urban centres further afield gradually made their mark on the provincial cities along the distant frontiers of the Empire. The force of Christianity that radiated out from Constantinople in the middle of the 4th century was soon felt at Jerash and the other Decapolis cities, most notably in the religious art and architecture that has been passed down to us in the many churches of the Byzantine era.

Historians are not certain of when Christianity became the official religion at Jerash. The lands east of the Jordan were certainly in contact with, and even accommodated, small Christian communities as early as the 3rd century. We know this from Roman literary references to Arabian bishops and dioceses in the early 3rd century. Shortly after the Emperor Constantine declared Christianity the offical religion of the Eastern Empire, bishops represented Jerash at the Council of Seleucia (359) and the Council of Chalcedon (451). In the late 4th century Epiphanius records that the citizens of Jerash celebrated annually the Christian miracle of Cana, at which water was turned into wine. This ritual probably took place at the fountain that now stands within the Fountain Court, in the centre of a complex of several large churches.

For some 300 years, the former Roman provinces of Arabia and Syria were part of the Byzantine Empire. Like Rome before it, Byzantium experienced fluctuating fortunes, with periods of prosperity alternating with decades of decline, all of which was reflected in the architecture of the cities.

The area of modern Jordan continued to live off the combination of transit trade, agriculture and industry. For most of the 4th and 5th centuries, the area's population increased, as attested by the archaeological remains of substantial towns and villages throughout the land, combined with traces of wide-spread agricultural acitivity. The fortified frontier zone, the *limes arabicus*, appears to have reached its height from the years of Diocletian to the death of Theodosius II, or the period 284–450. In the 5th and 6th centuries, most of the frontier forts were abandoned, as local security may have passed increasingly into the hands of Arab tribes.

The major new buildings in Jerash in the 4th and 5th centuries were churches, most of which were constructed with re-used stones from earlier Roman monuments. Fifteen churches have been discovered at Jerash to date, and more are probably still covered by earth, waiting to be excavated and studied. Most of the churches were built in the 5th and 6th centuries, particularly at the time when the Emperor Justinian (527–565) briefly revived the city's fortunes.

By the early 7th century, richly decorated churches were meeting the pastoral needs of a community that was physically and politically in decline. The area of old Roman Jerash had shrunk considerably; former shops and public monuments, particularly in the northern part of the city, were being used as stores or stables. The North Theatre seems to have ceased functioning as a theatre by the 5th century, when its stones were liberally scavenged for use in other parts of the city. Jerash was now a troubled city. It was vulnerable to the conquests of foreign forces because of the virtual disappearance of the former Roman frontier defensive zone along the edge of the deserts to the east and south. Those foreign forces were not long in coming.

THE ISLAMIC ERA

The Persian invasion of 614 and the occupation of the city until 630 was a hard blow that left Jerash even weaker still. The Byzantine period in Jordan finally came to an end in the early decades of the 7th century, when the forces of Islam came out of Arabia. They first clashed with the armies of Byzantium at Mu'tah, in south Jordan, in 629. The Byzantines won that battle, but in August 636 the Islamic forces invaded Jordan once again and finally defeated the Byzantines at the Battle of Yarmouk, in north Jordan.

The Byzantine era in Jordan came to an end as the Islamic forces marched on to Damascus and established the Umayyad Caliphate. Jerash, like the rest of the former cities of the Decapolis and the inhabitants of Jordan, Syria and Palestine, was suddenly part of the new Islamic Empire. Once again, as had happened so many times before in its history, the people and city of Jerash would be ruled and influenced by another foreign power and new ideas from abroad.

By this time the all-important regional and international trade routes had shifted away from Jerash and central Jordan towards Egypt and its Mediterranean and Red Sea ports. The lucrative spice and incense route from the Far East, India and southern Arabia also lost its importance. Suddenly finding themselves distant from both the power centres and the trade routes of the region, Jerash and other Romano–Byzantine cities had to adapt their economic bases to the new reality. The cities earned more of their income from agriculture and trading locally-produced industrial goods, such as glass and pottery. Jerash may have had a population of several thousand people, relying heavily on the income generated from the city's role as a market town for the surrounding agricultural belt. Coins from this period found at Jerash come from Damascus, Ramleh, Beisan and Tiberias, indicating widespread regional commercial contacts with the neighbouring provinces of Palestine and Damascus.

Recent excavations in the southern half of the city, near the South Decumanus and the Oval Plaza, have revealed a substantial Umayyad residential quarter. In the northern part of the city, in and around the former North Theatre, an Umayyad industrial complex has been excavated, including a series of large kilns for pottery making. The residential complexes at Jerash include standard early Islamic stone houses, very similar to those in the large Umayyad residential quarter recently discovered at Pella, in the north Jordan Valley. All evidence points to a good standard of living for a population that was comfortable, though probably not wealthy, with substantial local agriculture and industry, and extensive trading contacts with the adjacent provinces. The one Umayyad mosque discovered at Jerash to date is not at all a grand structure, in line with the lack of other signs of public wealth in Umayyad Jerash. The rich landowners or traders of the period probably moved to more important commercial and political centres such as Damascus, Tiberias or Ramleh, thus denying Jerash the fruits of their wealth and civic-minded generosity.

So little scholarship had been done on Umayyad Jerash during the first part of this century that most people readily accepted the old assumption that the city was a neglected, largely deserted little town in the 7th and 8th centuries. Recent excavations at Jerash and other early Islamic cities in Umayyad Jordan have radically changed our knowledge of that period. Far from abandoned, Jerash continued to exist and perhaps even develop slightly during the century of the Umayyad caliphate. While nothing to compare with the size or splendour of the former Roman city, Umayyad Jerash was nevertheless a significant regional city that, for example, minted its own coins and traded widely in the area.

By the middle of the 8th century, however, the end really was very near for this city that had already experienced over a thousand years of uninterrupted life. The assumption of power by the Abbasid dynasty and the transfer of the seat of the Islamic Caliphate from Damascus to Baghdad in 750 distanced Jerash yet further from the centre of power. A series of devastating earthquakes throughout the early and mid-8th century was the final blow. Many buildings were destroyed, and the few diehards who still lived among the destruction finally gave up the city for good.

Visitors wandered in and out of the debris during the following centuries. Some permanent habitation continued into the early Abbasid years. Even in the 13th and 14th centuries, in the Mamluke era, the substantial ruins of Jerash occasionally played host to groups of people who lived there for one reason or another, as evidenced by Mamluke pottery excavated around the North Theatre, the Oval Plaza and other parts of the city.

THE REDISCOVERY OF JERASH

In early 1806, the daring German scholar and traveller Ulrich Jasper Seetzen was the first European to stumble upon Jerash. He set out from Aleppo to explore the lands of southern Syria and the region of the Decapolis, and correctly identified the ruins of Jerash as those of ancient Gerasa, one of the decapolitan towns.

In May 1812, the Anglo-Swiss explorer John Lewis Burckhardt visited Jerash for a few hours on a journey from Tripoli to Cairo, sponsored by the London-based Association for Promoting the Discovery of the Interior Parts of Africa. The English traveller James Silk Buckingham was the next European to visit Jerash and record his observations. He documented many of the city's individual monuments in 1816.

Two more Englishmen visited Jerash in March 1818. Both Commanders of the Royal Navy, C.L. Irby and J. Mangles visited several of the Decapolis cities, spending a week at Jerash and documenting many of its most imposing structures. Eight years later, the French nobleman the Marquis Leon de Laborde visited the city with the engraver Linant, who made the first professional drawings of the ruins.

In 1867, Lt Charles Warren of the Royal Engineers set off from Jerusalem to survey the area east of the Jordan River, under the aegis of the two-year-old Palestine Exploration Fund. He spent about three days at Jerash, taking some of the earliest photographs of the ruins. In 1880–81 Lt C.R. Conder was charged by the Palestine Exploration Fund with leading a survey team to eastern Palestine, but the Ottoman government refused to allow the expedition to proceed, and the effort was aborted after only a brief foray into the Amman area. Lt Conder, however, accompanied Prince Albert Victor and Prince George on a tour of the Holy Land, during which they visited Jerash on 13 April, 1882.

Several years later, the Palestine Exploration Fund sponsored a surface survey of Jordan by the German Gottlieb Schumacher who produced the most thorough and serious scholarship on the ancient city. By that time, however, Jerash was no longer a deserted ruin. In 1878, the Ottoman government had installed a small community of Circassians, as it did at many other village sites throughout the lands east of the Jordan. The original Circassian community expanded over time, giving rise to the modern city of Jerash that now overlooks the ruins from the east.

By the turn of the last century, serious scholarship on Jerash and the other antiquities of Jordan and Palestine was well under way. The German team of Brunnow and Von Domaszewski produced their authoritative, three-volume study entitled *Die Provincia Arabia*, published between 1904 and 1909. In the early 1920s, after the establishment of the Emirate of Transjordan, the English Professor John Garstang carried out research and some consolidation, conservation and restoration work at Jerash, during his stint as the first director of the new Jordanian Department of Antiquities.

The most extensive archaeological excavation and architectural research at Jerash was done in a six-year period starting in 1928, by a joint Anglo-American team sponsored by Yale University, the British School of Archaeology in Jerusalem, and the American Schools of Oriental Research. The results of their work were edited by Professor Carl H. Kraeling and published in 1938 in a monumental book entitled *Gerasa, City of the Decapolis*, which remains the standard reference work for writers and scholars on the city. The most recent comprehensive study, Iain Browning's *Jerash and the Decapolis*, was published in 1982.

Considerable work has been done over the last fifty years by many individuals and teams from throughout the world, co-ordinated by the Jordanian Department of Antiquities. The department has also been responsible for conservation and restoration work at Jerash, much of which was carried out under the late Gerald Lankester Harding, the former director of the Department of Antiquities. After his death in 1979 he was buried, as he had requested, inside the Roman city walls of Jerash, in the south-western corner of the ruins near the Mortuary Church.

The Shrine of St Mary (see p. 109)

PART TWO

Visiting Jerash and the Cities of the Decapolis

Jerash's great popularity as a tourist site stems from both the richness of its ruins and its convenient location near Amman and the other major urban centres in the northern part of the country. Jerash is a forty-five-minute drive by car from Amman, along the main road to north Jordan that is currently being transformed in stages into a four-lane dual carriageway. Regular taxi and bus services are available to Jerash from the Abdali station in Amman. Travel agencies and the major hotels throughout Jordan can arrange sightseeing trips for small groups in cars, or for larger groups in buses. English-speaking guides, trained and supervised by the government, are always available at the Jerash Visitors' Centre, which also includes an adjacent restaurant and snack bar with an outdoor terrace, rest rooms, post office, telephone, descriptive literature, a lounge area, the tourist police office, a shop for small souvenirs and films, a few display cases with some of the artefacts excavated in Jerash over the years, and a scale model of the ruins today. The restaurant is open daily from 8.00 a.m. to 9.00 p.m. Entry into the ruins is 250 fils for Jordanians, and one dinar for others. In the adjacent modern city of Jerash, visitors can find any other required services, including medical care, shops, banks, restaurants, taxis and buses. There are no international class hotels in Jerash, because the city is so close to Amman, where most visitors to Jordan stay. A three-star hotel is located about twenty minutes west of Jerash, near the Arab castle of Qala'at al-Rabad and the village of Ajloun. A Jerash sound-and-light show, in English, Arabic, French and German, starts every evening after sunset, or around 8.00 p.m., from May to October. The JETT bus company in Amman (telephone 664146) offers transport to the sound-and-light show every evening.

For two weeks in July or August, the city of Jerash blazes with life and light during the Jerash Festival for Culture and Arts, the single largest festival of its kind in the Middle East. It includes booths, where dozens of Jordanian craftsmen and women display their handicrafts and also demonstrate their production techniques, along with a book fair, exhibitions of Jordanian fine arts, and nightly shows by the best local, Arab, and international performing artists in such fields as music, singing, dance, poetry, theatre, acrobatics and film. The festival takes place in late July or August, and lasts for two weeks, opening every day from mid-afternoon to midnight.

In 1982, the Department of Antiquities launched the Jerash International Project as a five-year programme of excavation and restoration, aiming to have teams from ten countries working simultaneously in different parts of the city. At its height in 1982–3, eight different teams working in Jerash represented Jordan, the United States, France, Great Britain, Australia, Italy, Poland and Spain. Most excavation was suspended in early 1984 because of budgetary constraints, after nearly two years of digging. Only a few areas of the city are still being excavated today, such as the Temple of Artemis and the Agora. Restoration work continues on schedule, however.

SUGGESTED ITINERARIES

The city is at its best in the early morning or the late afternoon, particularly in the spring, summer and autumn. Temperatures at these times of the day are cool, and the sun is lower in the sky, making for easier walking, some dramatic shadows in the Oval Plaza area, and better photography. Jerash is easily visited on a half-day or full-day tour from Amman, or combined with visits to other Decapolis cities in north Jordan. The Decapolis cities in Jordan with the most substantial ruins, and definitely worth a visit, are ancient Philadelphia (Amman), Gerasa (Jerash), Gadara (Umm Qais) and Pella (Tabaqat Fahl). All the Decapolis cities in north Jordan are within a two-hour drive from Amman. The furthest north is Gadara, north-west of the city of Irbid and about two hours by car from Amman. Near it, just north-east of Irbid, is Abila, about ninety minutes from Amman by car; but it offers few ruins to see above ground, because excavations at this site have only been in progress for a short time. Pella, near the modern village of Tabaqat Fahl in the northern Jordan Valley, is also a ninety-minute drive from Amman.

Decapolis enthusiasts pressed for time can see three of the cities in one day, if they are prepared for a long but exciting day with much driving and walking around Roman ruins. To do this, set off from Amman very early in the morning and drive north, stopping at Jerash for two hours, continuing to Gadara for a visit and a picnic lunch, and returning to Amman via Pella and the Jordan Valley in the late afternoon. Jerash and Gadara are more easily combined into a full day's trip, starting at Gadara early in the morning, then returning to Jerash for lunch at midday, followed by a walk around the ruins in the afternoon. How to visit the ruins of Jerash will depend on the degree of your interest and the amount of time at your disposal. You can see the entire city properly in a full day. Following are three suggested itineraries:

A full day's visit:
Arrive in the morning, and start at the South Gate. Walk up the South Street, through the Oval Plaza and into the Cardo. Walk straight up the entire length of the Cardo to the North Gate, taking in the monuments directly on the Cardo, such as the Agora and the Nymphaeum. Return via the North Tetrapylon to the North Theatre complex. Return via the North Tetrapylon to the West Baths, and from there to the Propylaeum Church area, from where you follow the route of the ancient city's Sacred Way, across the Cardo and up into the Temple of Artemis complex. After the Temple of Artemis, visit the complex of Byzantine churches directly to its south and west, including as many as you wish to see of the churches of Bishop Genesius, SS Cosmas and Damian, St John the Baptist, St George and the Synagogue Church. From south of the Temple of Artemis complex, walk down the Stepped Street, past the museum, through the Sarapion Passage, and into the area of the Church of St Theodore, the Fountain Court and the Cathedral. Descend the steps through the Cathedral Gate into the Cardo, and walk back to the rest house for lunch. After lunch, walk back to the South Tetrakionion and turn left up the South Decumanus to visit the restored Umayyad

House. Return via the Cardo to see the Oval Plaza, the Temple of Zeus complex, the South Theatre and the South Gate area, and walk or drive to Hadrian's Arch, where you can also see the Hippodrome and the Church of Bishop Marianos. If you have the time and interest, take a stroll through the modern city in the late afternoon, and return to the ruins for the sound and light show in the early evening.

A half-day's visit:
If you have only half a day to visit Jerash, walk through the South Gate to the Oval Plaza and the Cardo, and up the Cardo until the North Tetrapylon. Turn left and walk up the North Decumanus to the North Theatre complex, and from there to the Temple of Artemis. From the temple, go down the Stepped Street, through the Sarapion Passage and into the Fountain Court. Pass through the Cathedral and down the steps via the Cathedral Gate into the Cardo. Walk down the Cardo, turn right at the South Tetrakionion and walk up the South Decumanus to see the restored Umayyad house. Return via the South Tetrakionion to see the South Theatre and the Zeus Temple complex, and on your way back to Amman stop for a moment to see Hadrian's Arch and the Hippodrome.

A brief visit:
Some people have only an hour or two to stop at Jerash on their way along the main highway between Amman, Irbid and Damascus. If so, a brief visit is better than none at all. If you have only one or two hours to see the city, walk through the South Gate to the Oval Plaza, and up the Cardo to the Cathedral Gate. Pass through the Cathedral Gate to see the Cathedral and the Fountain Court, then walk through the Sarapion Passage and up the Stepped Street to reach the Temple of Artemis complex. From there walk through the North Theatre complex, and down the North Decumanus to the North Tetrapylon, returning down the Cardo to the Oval Plaza, the South Theatre and the South Gate.

PART THREE

The Monuments of Jerash

GROUP 1

HADRIAN'S ARCH

Hadrian's Arch

Hadrian's Arch, or the Triumphal Arch, is the first monument of Jerash that most people see as they approach the city from the south, on the main road from Amman. It stands alone, 460 metres south of the Jerash city walls next to the south-eastern end of the Hippodrome. It was built in the year AD 129/130 to honour the visit to Jerash of the Emperor Hadrian, who travelled widely throughout the whole Empire. The precise date is known from the dedicatory inscription found on the inside, north, face of the arch. The Gerasa municipal authorities built the arch so far outside the city, it seems, because they planned to extend the city walls outwards to meet the arch, whose untrimmed side walls would have bonded with the new city walls. The arch would then have served as a city gate, with both defensive and aesthetic functions. The arch and the adjacent Hippodrome have the same axis, and were obviously designed to relate to one another. A recently excavated street runs through the central doorway of the arch in a straight line to the south gate of the city. The salient architectural and decorative features of Hadrian's Arch are repeated in the South Gate, further indicating they were built at approximately the same time.

The arch has two parts: the triple-arched main structure, and the two pavilions at either end which were added at a later date. The entire structure is 37.45 metres long and 9.25 metres wide, and originally stood 21.5 metres high. Typical of the triumphal arches of the mid-2nd century AD, it has a large central passageway 10.8 metres high flanked by two smaller ones, each 5.2 metres high. The nearly identical north and south facades included four engaged half-columns on high pedestals, which framed three passages with wooden doors. Over the smaller side-passages are two recessed niches flanked by flat pilasters, with two more small flanking columns standing on the wedge-shaped brackets projecting from under the niches. Like the rest of the arch, the niches were elaborately carved and decorated with rich floral designs that have survived well.

The two large side pavilions were added at a later date to buttress the arch, when it became obvious that the city walls would not be expanded outwards to link up with it, perhaps towards the end of the 2nd or the start of the 3rd century. The pavilions have semicircular niches framed by pilasters on the south face, and were entered through small doorways on the north face.

THE CHURCH OF BISHOP MARIANOS

About fifty metres north of Hadrian's Arch and ten metres east of the Hippodrome wall is the Church of Bishop Marianos, one of three Byzantine churches discovered in Jerash in recent years. Built in AD 570, when the adjacent Hippodrome was in ruins, it nestles among a series of Byzantine tombs cut into the ground on both sides. The church was discovered and excavated in 1982–3 by Mr Ali Musa of the Jordanian Department of Antiquities and Dr Michael Gawlikowski of the University of Warsaw, Poland. They suggest, from the church's location and some inscriptional evidence, that it may have been used for memorial services for the dead who were buried in the nearby tombs. It was a normal feature of Greco–Roman cities to have tombs strewn on both sides of the main roads leading in and out of them. This was probably the case here, and the Byzantine inhabitants of Jerash added the church while continuing to use the former Roman cemetery.

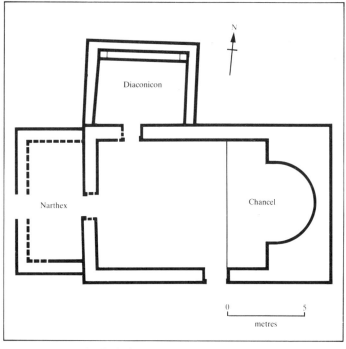

The Church of Bishop Marianos (*after Antoni Ostrasz*)

This relatively small church measures 13.5 by 8.1 metres on the outside and has walls 80 centimetres in width plastered on the inside. The interior of the church includes a central nave and an apse, to which were added a *diaconicon* in the north-west corner, and a *narthex* at the entrance. The *narthex*, or entrance passage, projects forward to the edge of the road that connected Hadrian's Arch with the South Gate, passing between the church and the Hippodrome.

A raised chancel traversed the width of the church on a 25-centimetre-high step in front of the apse. Four holes in the floor of the apse supported the legs of the altar. The apse was surrounded by two steps, in the centre of which the bishop's seat was located. Wooden benches ran along the north and south walls of the church, which was entered by a door in each of the west and south walls.

Mosaics with geometric patterns and crosses covered the floor of the church. The *diaconicon*, measuring 3.4 by 4.7 metres, was a chapel where the Eucharistic offerings were inspected. It was entered through a door in the nave wall. A 90-centimetre-high column near the east wall supported a marble slab which served as an altar. The *narthex*, the only one of its kind in Jerash's fifteen churches, is a room leading into the main western entrance of the church. It is slightly narrower than the nave and is just off centre in alignment.

Directly across the street from the church, within the walls of the former Hippodrome, are three rooms that served as the deacon's house. They were established within the existing Hippodrome walls soon after the church itself, and one of the rooms had a mosaic floor (now reburied) with three small prayer inscriptions. The arch over the entrance of the middle room is still in place.

The church was used into the 8th century, according to the excavated pottery, and was abandoned after destruction caused by an earthquake. Its valuable religious artefacts were cleaned out by the parishioners of the time. It provides further proof that a Christian community continued to live in Jerash well into the Umayyad period. The deacon's house was abandoned earlier, probably in the first half of the 7th century. Among the most interesting finds inside the church was a bronze chandelier that held four glass stem lamps and was suspended from the roof by four chains 30 centimetres long. Two such chandeliers flanked the chancel of the church.

THE HIPPODROME

Immediately north of Hadrian's Arch is the badly ruined Hippodrome, the sporting and entertainment centre of Roman Jerash. Impressive as it may be because of its size, the Hippodrome is also an enigma because we know neither when it was built nor whether it was ever completed or even used.

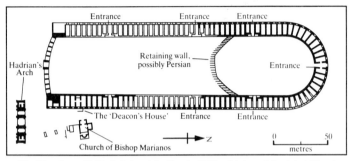

The Hippodrome, Hadrian's Arch and the Church of Bishop Marianos (*after Antoni Ostrasz*)

The Hippodrome is shaped like an elongated oval. It measures 244.5 metres long on the inside and varies in width from 51.28 metres at the northern end to 49.49 metres at the southern end. Its external dimensions are 261.42 metres long and an average 76.08 metres wide, and its external wall rose about 10 metres above the outside ground level. Though a large structure for Jerash, this is a rather small hippodrome compared with others in the more important political and commercial cities of the Roman Empire, such as Antioch.

The limestone blocks used to build the Hippodrome would have been a dazzling white when first installed. Like other large functional structures of its kind the Hippodrome had a simple exterior finish which included only decorative carving. The sixteen rows of seats built on a series of stepped arches would have accommodated up to 15,000 spectators, who entered the arena through at least six doors in the east and west outer walls. The preserved main entrance in the semicircular north wall led onto a ramp which may have been used by horses, camels and chariots. Just west of the northern entrance, above the three-metre-high podium wall, are the few remaining original stone seats that would have covered the entire interior of the *cavea*, or auditorium. The southern end of the Hippodrome included eleven stalls flanked by two large corner towers. The central stall, wider and taller than the other ten stalls, may have served as an entrance from the south.

The Hippodrome is built into the east side of a small valley, which required the construction of a high substructure to hold up the long western wall. Immediately east of the western wall is a depression, 10 metres deep and 100 metres long, which was artificially filled in when the Hippodrome was first built to produce a level arena where the popular races and sporting contests took place. But the substructure finally collapsed in antiquity and the erosion of the fill returned the depression to its natural state. At some later time, a semicircular retaining wall was built across the Hippodrome, approximately one third of the way down from the northern end, making the northern part of the arena usable once again. Some scholars suggest this was done in the brief Persian occupation of Jerash (AD 614–30) to transform the flat northern part of the Hippodrome into a polo field, but archaeologists who have studied the Hippodrome more recently question this theory.

Scholars also disagree about the dating of the Hippodrome, and about whether or not it was ever finished or inaugurated. The three different schools of thought argue, respectively, that it was designed and built in the late 1st century AD, well before Hadrian's Arch was constructed; that it was built roughly at the same time as the arch, around 129–30; or that it was built much later than the arch, at the end of the 2nd or early 3rd century. Lack of inscriptional evidence from within the Hippodrome keeps this argument very much alive.

THE TOMBS

It was standard practice in Greco–Roman cities to bury the dead in cemeteries that were first located along the main roads in and out of the city, but that usually expanded with time to surround the city completely. This is the case at Jerash, where different kinds of tombs have been discovered on all sides of the city.

The wealthier upper classes often built elaborate, above-ground tombs or mausolea to honour their dead. Most of these were long ago destroyed, the remaining examples being the

Tomb of Germanus north of the city, the tomb near the Visitors' Centre, the tomb just outside the North-West Gate, and foundations just before Hadrian's Arch, along the road from Amman to Jerash.

The more common tombs were chambers cut down into the rock, usually entered through a flight of steps. Several of these tomb chambers are visible on both sides of the main road into Jerash, near Hadrian's Arch. They were exposed when the modern road was built. Others have been excavated on both sides of the Church of Bishop Marianos, and in the South-West Cemetery, in the hills some 250 metres west of Hadrian's Arch.

While the tombs varied slightly in their size, settings and internal arrangement, they were entered usually through a staircase ending in a wide landing, leading down one step through a door into the main burial chamber. Some tombs were sealed with a single-slab stone door, others simply with rubble masonry. From a roughly rectangular main chamber, narrow burial recesses radiated out into the tomb walls. Most bodies were simply placed in the recesses, with only a few of the more important individuals buried in stone sarcophagi.

The few tombs excavated to date span the period from the 1st to the 6th centuries. Some of the tombs have been re-used constantly ever since as dwellings, stables or storage areas.

GROUP 2

THE CITY WALLS

The Roman city of Jerash was encircled by a thick, handsome wall that can still be traced around almost the entire city, though it is badly ruined in most places. The first city wall, excavated and studied by a French team near the South Gate, was 1.75 metres wide, or just over half the width of the existing wall. It was first laid out in the middle of the 1st century, around AD 60–70, only to be rebuilt, strengthened and altered in places over the ensuing centuries. The existing wall, best preserved near the South Gate, is a 4th-century late Roman or Byzantine structure.

The city walls, near the South Gate

The wall is three metres thick and uniformly built using the alternating headers-and-stretchers technique, though its height varies according to the terrain. It is regularly broken at intervals of 17–22 metres by six-metre-square towers integrally built into it. More than 100 towers once existed and two such towers, on either side of the South Gate, can be appreciated as you enter the city. The entire wall circuit extends for 3456 metres, enclosing an area of some 847,000 square metres on both sides of the River Chrysorhoas. The river passed through the city centre and provided a secure water supply, though how its entrance through the north walls was protected remains a mystery. The river left the city on the south side through the Watergate, a sluice defended by two large towers set against the river bed at oblique angles. This directed the water under some pressure into a narrow channel that spilled out of the city over a ten-metre-high waterfall. Very little remains to be seen of the original Watergate or the walls and towers in this area.

THE SOUTH GATE

Visitors today enter the ruins of ancient Jerash through the South

Gate, a few steps beyond the Visitors' Centre and Restaurant complex. The small structure between the Restaurant and the South Gate is another of the many Roman tombs that dotted the outskirts of the city. The existing tomb is a Byzantine construction over an earlier Roman structure that may have been a tomb or perhaps served some other function.

The design and decoration of the South Gate are virtually identical with Hadrian's Arch, and the two structures are perfectly lined up with each other to allow the road from Philadelphia (Amman) to pass through them both on its way into the city of Jerash. The South Gate, therefore, is assumed to date from the same period as the arch, or around AD 129–30. It was excavated in the 1930s, and its immediate vicinity has been studied since 1983 by a French team under the direction of Monsieur Jacques Seigne, as part of the Jerash International Project.

The South Gate

The existing gate was built over the remains of an earlier, simpler gate with a single passageway measuring just 2.65 metres wide. It dated probably from the second half of the 1st century AD, when the original city wall was first built, and stood a few metres west of the present gate, on the same line. The South Gate,

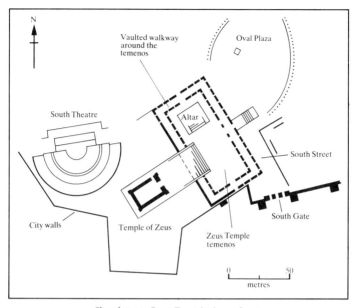

Plan of sites in Group Two (*after Jacques Seigne*)

like Hadrian's Arch, has a large central passageway 4.2 metres wide between two smaller passageways 2.32 metres wide. The entire structure is flanked by two pavilions bonded to the gate and forming an integral part of it, but these were not later additions like the pavilions around Hadrian's Arch. The south faces of the pavilions have simple niches, while the north faces have doors leading into interior chambers within the gate. The three passageways are flanked by four engaged columns on pedestals that still sport the beautiful, though unusual acanthus foliate carving, paralleled by similar but less intricate carving on Hadrian's Arch. The gate complex is on the line of the city wall, in between two large protruding towers, built in the later Byzantine period, giving the false impression that it is set back from the line of the wall.

Recent excavations by the French team immediately inside the west side of the South Gate have produced a complete stratigraphic record of the use of this part of the city. Pottery evidence shows that the earliest human activity here dates from the Middle Bronze Age (around 1500 BC) and the Early Iron Age (1200–1100 BC). The earliest architectural remains are a Hellenistic floor level from the 2nd century BC, followed by the first major construction phase of Roman Jerash in the middle of the 1st century AD. Most of the early Roman material is from around AD 40–50, corresponding to the archaeological and inscriptional evidence that dates the lower platform of the adjacent Zeus Temple complex to the same period. The foundations and a doorway from the original, 1.75-metre-thick, city wall were also revealed under the west side of the existing South Gate.

Third-century olive press, just inside the South Gate

The area immediately to the left after passing through the South Gate was a market place in the late 2nd and 3rd centuries AD. In an underground room at the south-west corner of this area are the remains of a 3rd-century olive press partly constructed from re-used capitals and column bases. The room containing the press was roofed with wood, over which a two-storey house/shop complex once stood. The row of column bases visible today formed a portico that separated the market area from the South

Street which linked the South Gate with the Oval Plaza. The market area was destroyed towards the end of the 3rd century when a thick wall was built, separating it from the street. It was then used as a defensive zone, with a central courtyard surrounded by five rooms whose plan is still clear today. This probably housed the soldiers who manned the tower adjacent to the South Gate, and who gained access to the tower and the city walls through the internal staircase visible west of the gate. The drain running through the area was also an early 4th-century structure contemporary with the new city walls that stand today. Visible throughout this area are the later walls as rebuilt in the Byzantine period. In the 5th century AD, a small marketplace flourished just inside the South Gate; the same area seems to have accommodated a potter's workshop in the 6th century, according to the research of the French archaeologists who excavated, studied and restored the area.

THE SOUTH STREET

The short, uphill walk from the South Gate to the Oval Plaza follows the path of the ancient South Street. To the right as you walk up the street are the remains of two recently excavated walls, both on a north–south axis and three metres apart. The first wall was the eastern boundary of the street, and has been rebuilt at least once since early Roman days. The inner wall appears to be the western side of a large public building lying unexcavated underneath the hillside. Excavations here to a depth of five metres have yet to hit bed-rock, and have produced a well stratified sequence of pottery going back to the Hellenistic period of the 2nd and 1st centuries BC. Many scholars are convinced that the first Hellenistic city of Jerash, dating from at least the 2nd century BC, was located on this hill, which is now occupied by the old restaurant and snack bar. Only further excavations higher up the hill will confirm this theory.

Dr Asem N. Barghouti of the University of Jordan, who excavated this area in the late 1970s, suggests the approach from the South Gate to the Plaza may have been divided into two parts: a staircase for pedestrians entered through the central and small eastern passageways of the South Gate, and a sloping ramp for vehicles or mounted riders entered through the small western passageway, whose threshold has the most pronounced wheel marks. The central passageway, which also has some wheel marks, may have been used by pedestrians, vehicles, and mounted riders.

Excavations near the South Gate have produced the earliest artefacts of human occupation in Jerash, dating from the Middle Bronze and Early Iron Ages, or from around 1500 to 1100 BC, confirming that the area around the South Street is probably the oldest part of Jerash. If future excavations confirm that the first Hellenistic settlement was on or around the hill east of the South Street, relating to the early Hellenistic sanctuary that was probably located in the area of the Temple of Zeus to the west, then the short and humble South Street will prove to have been one of Jordan's more venerable and ancient pathways. Half-way up the street, on the left, are clearly visible the vaults supporting the lower courtyard, or *temenos*, of the Zeus Sanctuary complex.

THE ZEUS SANCTUARY COMPLEX

On the large hill to your left as you walk up the South Street to the Oval Plaza is the Zeus Sanctuary complex, with the Temple of Zeus itself crowning it all at the top of the hill. The area at first appears to be a confusing, tumbled mess of collapsed stones, column drums, bases and capitals, sections of vaults, pieces of reconstructed and original walls, scattered bits of carved stone, and the odd inscription. In fact, the Zeus complex was a highly sophisticated architectural and engineering feat that was neatly laid out to emphasise the temple structure at its summit.

Recent research by a French team, combined with previous work by Jordanian and foreign teams since the 1920s, has resolved many questions. The existing temple was built in AD 162–3 on the same spot as an earlier 1st-century AD Roman sanctuary. Inscriptions found here recount that when the first Roman temple to Zeus was being constructed in the first half of the 1st century AD, substantial gifts of money to help finance it were made in AD 22–3 and 42–3 by Zabdion and Aristonas, the sons of Aristomachus, priest of Tiberius. It is also firmly believed that on this same hill there once stood a 1st or 2nd-century BC Hellenistic sanctuary, serving the earliest town at Jerash on Camp Hill across the Oval Plaza.

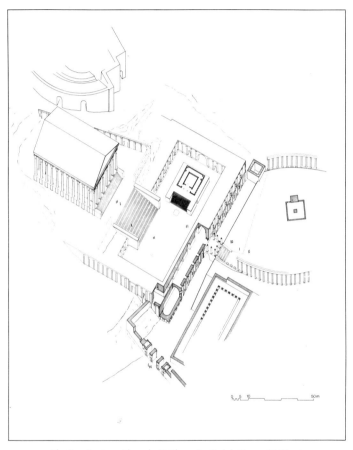

The Zeus Sanctuary (*drawn by G. Charpentier, R. de la Noue and J. Seigne*)

At the point where the South Street meets the paving of the Oval Plaza, a modest staircase on the left leads up to the *temenos*, the first of three successive terraces at different levels that make up the entire Zeus Sanctuary complex. The *temenos*, or sacred precinct associated with the temple, measures some 100 metres by 50 metres in size, and is the largest of the three terraces. It was surrounded on all four sides by a vaulted walkway penetrated by three doors on the south, east and north. The eastern side of the *temenos* was supported by subterranean vaults that are best preserved under its eastern side, and are visible on the left as you walk up to the Oval Plaza from the South Gate. Some of the inner *temenos* wall has been reconstructed along the east side of the *temenos*, and shows the rather simple decorative work that adorned the entire wall.

In the northern half of the *temenos* terrace are the remains of a large 'altar', with its associated paving in front of it. This is believed to be part of the original sanctuary that was built in AD 40–50, according to the earlier archaeological and inscriptional evidence, confirmed in recent years by the French excavations along the foundations of the south-eastern corner of the *temenos* terrace walls.

The Temple of Zeus

A monumental, 28.25-metre-wide staircase on the west side of the *temenos* led to an upper terrace (now buried underneath earth and the collapsed temple columns) overlooking the central courtyard of the *temenos*. From here, the staircase continued up to the Temple of Zeus itself. The temple is built on a podium 41.25 metres long and 28.25 metres wide. It was surrounded on all four sides by Corinthian columns 14.84 metres high, eight each at the front and rear and twelve along each side. The front wall is 4.5 metres thick, to accommodate an internal staircase leading up to the roof. The front entrance leads into the simple main chamber, where decorative pilasters which divide the walls into panels may have carried metal capitals. Nothing remains of the actual shrine, which may have been located along the back of the temple, on a platform reached by a flight of steps. The north wall of the temple was pierced by a small door. The exterior walls of the temple are decorated only by eight semicircular niches between the columns on each side, and corner pilasters at the extremities. The temple on its upper terrace was surrounded again by a recently discovered smaller *temenos*, portions of whose pilastered north-western wall have been excavated.

THE SOUTH THEATRE

The South Theatre today is one of the most impressive of Jerash's public buildings, in part because of its extensive restoration. Begun at the end of the 1st century AD and completed in the early 2nd century, the theatre was partly financed by contributions from some of the city's wealthier citizens, who left inscriptions to mark their munificence for posterity. This was the larger of the city's two theatres, the other being the smaller North Theatre that started its life as an *odeon* (covered theatre), and possibly also served as the meeting hall for the city assembly.

The South Theatre is oriented in such a manner that the sun shines into spectators' eyes for only a brief period in the late afternoon. The *cavea* (semicircular auditorium) is divided into two halves, separated by a terrace running the full length of the *cavea* seating. The lower half was built into the side of the hill, while the top half was built up above it. The lower half of the *cavea* is divided by stairs into four sections of fourteen rows each, with numbers inscribed underneath each seat in the two outer sections.

The numbers are most clearly visible in the lowest seats along the western side of the auditorium. The upper *cavea* was similarly divided into eight sections with at least fifteen rows each, if not more, putting the theatre's total capacity at over 3000 people.

The South Theatre

Visitors today enter the theatre from the front through two arched passageways, or *paradoi*, that lead into the semi-circular orchestra. Three sets of stairs lead from the orchestra to the lower seats. The upper seats of the theatre were reached through four arched *vomitoria* entered from the back of the theatre. The stepped arches of these *vomitoria* help support the upper half of the auditorium.

The rather elaborately decorated stage has been restored and repaved, though the original may have had a wooden floor. The front of the stage is decorated wih pedimented and arched niches, with steps at either end leading up to the stage. The wall rising behind the stage, the *scaenae frons*, is pierced by three doors used by the performers to enter and exit the stage, along with two arched doorways also leading onto the stage from the sides. The highly decorated *scaenae frons* includes some of the same finely carved acanthus leaves and flutes found on the South Gate and Hadrian's Arch. The *scaenae frons* would have had a second storey repeating most of the decorative and architectural elements of the lower level. Much of the outer (north) wall of the theatre is a modern reconstruction.

THE OVAL PLAZA

The Oval Plaza, first dubbed the 'Forum' by Burckhardt in the early 19th century, is one of Jerash's most intriguing spaces both because of its shape, so rare in the ancient world, and its architectural and aesthetic function within the town plan. It was first investigated in the early 1930s, and has been the subject of scholarly study and speculation ever since.

The Oval Plaza

The Plaza was built in a natural depression that was considerably filled in by the Romans to provide an almost flat surface, though the Plaza floor still rises slightly towards the north. Measuring over 90 metres long and 80 metres wide, it is shaped like a skewed oval, and is ringed by a colonnade of Ionic columns mounted on small blocks and supporting an architrave. The columns are evenly spaced except at two points on the western side where the architrave is also slightly raised above the norm. Side streets entered the plaza at these two points, from residential and commercial districts that were excavated in the late 1970s by Dr Asem N. Barghouti of the University of Jordan. Immediately north-west of the Plaza he uncovered streets and residential areas that had been inhabited for over 1000 years, from the 2nd century BC to the 8th century AD. A related network of water and drainage channels from the west and south-west joined, and flowed into, the main city sewerage system at a point under the paving stones of the Oval Plaza. Immediately beside the Plaza colonnade is a 2.2-metre-wide sidewalk paved with irregularly laid stones. The entire central space is paved with heavy blocks that follow the elliptical curvature of the colonnades, except in two places. Along the very southern side of the Plaza the paving stones do not follow the curve of the colonnades, but are laid in a straight line that connects the two southern horns of the colonnades. This line is parallel with the axis of the Temple of Zeus complex on the hill directly above it, and helps explain the significance of the peculiar shape of the Oval Plaza. In the approximate centre of the Plaza are the foundation remains of a 9.5-metre-wide square structure in which the moulded footing of a pink limestone pedestal may have supported a statue (and now supports a column erected for the Jerash festival). When the Plaza lost its original Roman function and fell into decay, it was built over in many areas. In the late 7th century, a water tank, or perhaps even a fountain, was built around the central square structure. Water reached it through ceramic pipes buried in two lines beneath the original paving stones. Their lines can be traced today, entering the centre of the Plaza from the north and west. One of the walls of the water tank seems to have incorporated a series of stone seats; the remains of nine of these are still near their original position, one even sporting an arm-rest. The area was abandoned in the 8th century and gradually filled up.

Excavations and clearing work revealed what C.S. Fisher in the 1930s suggested were base stones for a triple archway at the junction of the Oval Plaza and the Cardo, the colonnaded main street of Jerash that runs northwards from the north end of the Plaza. Such a Corinthian-style triple archway, the width of the Cardo, may have been added in the 2nd century AD, well after the Plaza was built in the 1st century. Note the Corinthian order of the Cardo columns, but the older Ionic colonnade in the Plaza.

Recent study of the Oval Plaza and the Cardo by Mr Warwick Ball, an Australian archaeologist, questions whether such an archway ever existed. Rather, he suggests, the base stones uncovered in the 1930s, and still in place today on both sides of the Cardo, were more likely to have supported terminal piers marking the end of the Cardo colonnade, as was done at the end of the North Decumanus, where it intersects with the Cardo.

The purpose of the Oval Plaza has long been debated. The uncovering of an important public building on the west side of the Cardo, between the Plaza and the South Decumanus, may bring to light the true Forum, or Agora, of Jerash, the city's civic and business centre and key meeting place. It seems more likely now, as both G. Lankester Harding and Iain Browning have proposed, that the peculiar shape of the Oval Plaza was a brilliant architectural device that reconciled and visually linked the different axes of the Cardo and the Zeus Sanctuary complex to its south-west. Passing southwards from the end of the colonnaded and porticoed Cardo, a person would enter the large, open, sun-drenched Plaza and find his eyes following the flow of the eastern colonnade of the Plaza, finally leading his attention to the *temenos* and temple of the Zeus Sanctuary. Coming the other way, a person entering the Plaza from the South Street would be led gently northwards by the curvature of the colonnades towards the start of the Cardo. Inside the Cardo the more symmetrical city plan took over, where right angles and neatly intersecting axes prevailed.

THE CITY PLAN

By leaving the north end of the Oval Plaza and entering the Cardo Maximus, the main colonnaded street of ancient Gerasa, you also step into the more strict and formal city plan that is such an important aspect of Greco–Roman cities. Indeed, several scholars and architectural historians have seen the city planning of Jerash as its most important legacy to modern scholarship, for it represents a style of urban planning in the Arab east that included both Hellenistic and Roman concepts.

The basic grid layout of the city, first devised in the mid-1st century AD, seems deceptively simple. It centres on the 12-metre-wide Cardo, the colonnaded main street running in an approximate north–south direction for just over 800 metres; this is intersected at almost equal intervals by two colonnaded side streets 8 to 9 metres wide running in an east–west direction, the North Decumanus and South Decumanus. Between these major thoroughfares, a network of smaller side streets from 5 to 6.5 metres wide intersected with one another, and with the three major arteries of the city. This produced almost uniform, rectangular 'city blocks' that measured typically 120 metres by 50 metres, according to recent research in the south-western part of the city by Dr Asem Barghouti and the Jordanian Department of Antiquities. The city plan took advantage of the contours of the land, with the Cardo running along a terrace west of the river, the two *decumani* placed in natural east–west depressions, and the key religious monuments, the temples of Zeus and Artemis, sited on the crests of two hills, from where they could be seen from almost every part of the city.

Most of the important streets and public monuments were located in the western half of the city; the area east of the river had a few public monuments but was probably dominated by residential quarters. The layout of the North and South Decumani, Dr Barghouti suggests, aimed to define the huge religious sector of the Temple of Artemis and to emphasise focal points in other quarters of the city. He also notes that the city wall does not follow a rigid shape, but rather takes the form of 'a girdle loosely flung around' the city. The walls were pierced by a series of city gates, the best preserved today being the South Gate and the smaller North Gate. Two other gates, the North-West Gate and the South-West Gate, gave access to the city from the west, leading respectively into the North and South Decumani.

One of the anomalies in the otherwise regular plan of the city is the relationship of the axis of the Zeus Temple complex to the axis of the Cardo. The dilemma was ingeniously resolved by the peculiar form of the skewed Oval Plaza, which allowed the more east–west axis of the Temple of Zeus to be incorporated into the north–south layout of the rest of the city.

GROUP 3

THE CARDO

As you leave the Oval Plaza and start walking up the Cardo, the ruins start to take on a more human scale, perhaps if only because of the universal and timeless sensation of strolling down a city street or its sidewalks. But this was no ordinary street. Paved and colonnaded throughout and redesigned in parts several times throughout its life, the Cardo was the architectural and urban backbone of the city, the central axis to which all other thoroughfares and districts related. It measures just over 800 metres in length, from the North Gate of the city to the entrance of the Oval Plaza, and was conceived from the start, in the second half of the 1st century AD, as one architectural unit. It seems to have been built first as a single long street, uninterrupted by the two existing *decumani*. The original Ionic colonnades may have been added after the street was finished, in the late 1st or early 2nd century. Sometime in the 2nd century it was decided to widen the Cardo and replace its Ionic capitals with more

View along the Cardo, looking towards the Temple of Zeus

grandiose Corinthian capitals. This project seems to have started at the south end of the Cardo and worked its way northwards. Perhaps to save money for major public monuments such as the Temple of Artemis in the city centre, the work stopped at the intersection of the North Decumanus, where the North Tetrapylon was built around AD 165. The Cardo north of the North Tetrapylon retains its original, 1st-century AD street width and Ionic colonnade. The old Ionic colonnades from the rest of the Cardo were apparently re-used to build the colonnades along the North and South Decumani.

No two columns along the southern Cardo are identical; many have the original Ionic shafts and bases, with later Corinthian upper drums and capitals. The bases of the columns vary in diameter by up to 14 centimetres, as do the lengths of the lower, middle and upper drum pieces. The capitals also vary in height and diameter by up to 15 centimetres. The columns carried a continuous architrave which is well preserved along the western colonnade of the first stretch of the Cardo. The architrave was interrupted or raised to a higher level, with the addition of an entablature, when larger and wider Corinthian columns marked the entrance of an important public building; this can be seen clearly about half-way up the first stretch of the Cardo, between the Oval Plaza and the South Tetrakionion, where the architrave of the smaller columns rests on brackets protruding from the sides of their taller neighbours. The normal arrangement of the street included a sidewalk on both sides, from which steps led up to the covered porticoes, incorporated into the colonnades. In some places, a different arrangement is found. Two examples are the steps protruding onto the sidewalk in front of the Cathedral Gate and the Nymphaeum, where the porticoes are higher than usual above the street level and the street-facing wall of the portico is decorated with low niches; and the raised sidewalks in front of the Agora that are Byzantine work of the 6th century. The street is paved with diagonally-laid limestone blocks, which are smaller and more standard in size north of the North Tetrapylon, producing a more regular paving pattern. The kerb on both sides of the Cardo is pierced at regular intervals by small semi-circular openings; these allowed waste water to find its way along the surface of the street and through drains into the underground sewerage system that included a long drain underneath the length of the Cardo. The drain could be serviced through openings in the Cardo marked by round, stone man-hole covers. In many parts of the Cardo can be seen clearly the grooves in the paving stones formed by centuries of use by the metal wheels of Roman traffic.

THE AGORA

About half-way up the southern section of the Cardo, between the Oval Plaza and the South Tetrakionion, the regular run of the columns on the left-hand side of the street is suddenly interrupted by four large Corinthian columns that mark the entrance to an important public building. This area was jointly excavated in the late 1970s by the Department of Antiquities and Dr Asem Barghouti, and more recently by a Spanish team headed in turn by Dr Emilio Olavarri and Armando Fernandez.

The work has started to reveal an enormous structure behind the columns, measuring at least fifty metres square and bounded to the north and south by two small, five-metre-wide side streets that run into the Cardo. There are tantalizing clues that this may have been the focal point of the city's commercial affairs. Carved on the lower section of one of the four large columns is the Greek word 'Agora', after which the building has been tentatively named. The letters are rather poorly carved, however, suggesting they may be casual additions from a period considerably later than the original construction of the building. Passing through the four large columns, one enters a central portico with two free-standing columns *in antis* in front of a central monumental triple gateway whose main door measured 4.85 metres high. Flanking north and south porticoes (the north one paved with a now reburied geometric mosaic floor) led into a series of four two-storey *tabernae*, or shops, on either side of the main triple gateway. Recent excavations in the four northern *tabernae* have revealed an attractive mosaic floor in the northernmost shop. An inscription in the mosaic says it was built on the orders of a certain Aquilinus. The portrait of a man in the centre of the mosaic may be that of Aquilinus himself, who says he rebuilt the shop after he found it abandoned and destroyed. The date in the mosaic inscription is slightly damaged, but must be either AD 462–3 or 562–3. Mr Armando Fernandez, who supervised the work in the

Agora, believes the mosaic dates from the 6th century.

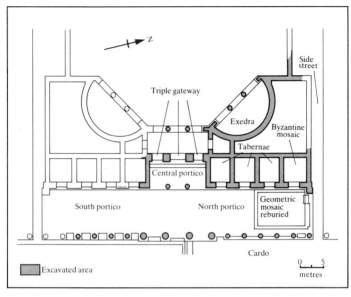

The 'Agora' (after Armando Fernandez)

Excavations inside the Agora have uncovered a complete *exedra*, or semicircular recess, with square pilasters at its corners and two free-standing columns between the pilasters. A wall from one of the *exedra*'s corner pilasters runs straight north to meet the side street, at one of the building's side entrances. The tops of columns sticking out of unexcavated ground in other parts of the building suggest that this important structure had four *exedrae* around its perimeter, inside which was an octagonal peristyle of free-standing columns. Drains running out to the Cardo and the street to the north indicate a large open interior or a fountain. The high sidewalk in front of the building, along both sides of the Cardo, was raised to its present level by the 6th-century Byzantine inhabitants of the city, most likely during the same reconstruction that saw the mosaic floor laid in the shop, either to enlarge the portico or to provide extra structural support for the huge portico columns. The Byzantine Gerasenes also placed the stone basin below the original Roman lion's head fountain at the north end of the sidewalk in front of the complex.

No inscriptions have been found to help date the original Roman building, whose excavators have used architectural evidence to propose a construction date in the second half of the 2nd century AD. An inscription near the fountain at the north end of the portico is dated 211, which would be the very latest date of its construction. Inscriptions on three of the columns on the Cardo said they were presented by 'people of the market', 'potters' and retail traders' guilds', and individuals, strengthening the theory that this was the Agora, or main commercial centre of the city.

Archaeological artefacts unearthed here included Iron Age (1200–550 BC) remains and a Hellenistic stone wall from the late 2nd or early 1st century BC, confirming the strong theory that the southern part of the city was where its earliest inhabitants lived and worked. The building is still being excavated and restored by the Spanish team working as part of the Jerash International Project, under the auspices of the Spanish Institute for History and Archaeology in Amman. It is not open to the public though it can be well appreciated from the level of the sidewalk above the Cardo.

THE SOUTH TETRAKIONION

The intersection of the Cardo and the South Decumanus is marked by the remains of a once towering and monumental piece of architecture, the South Tetrakionion. This was one of the several different kinds of *tetrapyla* that marked important street intersections in the Roman east; another kind found at Jerash is the North Tetrapylon, further up the Cardo at its intersection with the North Decumanus.

The South Tetrakionion started as a simple right-angle intersection of two streets and underwent considerable development and redesign. Perhaps in the middle of the 2nd century AD, four free-standing *tetrakionia* were erected in the centre of the intersection. Their bases are still there today, but in their original state each 4.1-metre-square base with decorative shell niches on each face supported four granite Corinthian columns standing on

The South Tetrakionion

square pedestals. Crowning the top of each set of four columns was a square, articulated entablature. The corners formed by the intersection of the two streets were occupied by assorted public and private buildings. A man-hole cover in the centre of the four podia gave access into the city's sewerage system, at the junction of two large drains beneath the Cardo and the South Decumanus. Sometime in the 3rd or 4th century AD, according to Kraeling, the square intersection was remodelled: the buildings in the corners were demolished and a huge circular plaza measuring 43.6 metres in diameter was developed around the four *tetrakionia*. But some scholars, such as Margaret Lyttelton, argue that the circular plaza and the Tetrakionion were both built at the same time, in the 2nd century AD. The paving stones of the plaza end against the curb of a 1.4-metre-wide walkway that went around the inside of the plaza, joining with and continuing the sidewalks of the intersecting streets. Each inside circular face of the four sides of the plaza was pierced by three doors leading into two-storey shops with upper-floor windows overlooking the plaza.

During the Byzantine period, considerable rebuilding took place in the rooms and buildings behind the facades of the plaza, in an area which seems to have continued to serve shops, workshops or domestic structures. By the early Islamic period of the 7th–8th centuries, the plaza seems to have lost its original monumental form, as the residents of Jerash built a small housing area around it, re-using many stones from earlier buildings.

THE SOUTH DECUMANUS

Intersecting with the Cardo at the South Tetrakionion is the South Decumanus, one of the two major colonnaded 'side streets' running in an east–west direction. The South Decumanus was first laid out as part of the 1st-century AD town plan; it was then colonnaded and repaved in its present configuration around AD 170, according to archaeological and coin evidence from earlier cisterns beneath the street, that were cut into when the street was built. Excavations further west of the street by University of Jordan archaeologists have turned up evidence of domestic structures spanning the thousand years from the Hellenistic to the Umayyad period. Thus an earlier street may have led once to the very first residential quarters of the city. The entire street on both sides of the South Tetrakionion slopes down from west to east, and the architrave carried on top of the columns slopes down with it.

The South Bridge, before recent reconstruction

The street crossed the River Chrysorhoas on the South Bridge, the only remaining one of the several ancient bridges that spanned the river. The remains of three of the bridge's original arches still stand over the river bed dividing the modern town from the ruins. The original width of the South Bridge can be imagined from the bridge's restored lower revetments. Its length, with its approaches, was 73 metres.

The bridge has recently been restored by a Department of Antiquities team headed by Professor H. Kalayan, who has also carried out restoration work during the past decade at the Temple of Zeus, the Nymphaeum, and elsewhere at Jerash.

THE UMAYYAD HOUSE

Immediately behind the northern columns (right-hand side) of the South Decumanus, about 115 metres west of the Cardo, is a large excavated area with a complex, tiered arrangement of walls, rooms, steps and corridors. This is a recently excavated and restored house from the Umayyad city of the 7th to 8th century, probably the best such example of an Umayyad house in Jordan.

The Umayyad House, with the South Decumanus in the background

Excavations here in 1982–3 by the Polish team of the Jerash International Project, under the leadership of Dr Michael Gawlikowski and architect Antoni Ostrasz, indicated the area was used continuously from early Roman to Abbasid days (from the 1st to the 9th centuries). Several underground cisterns and associated walls near the street date from the 1st and 2nd centuries AD, and probably formed part of the neighbourhood's public water system. Earlier Hellenistic and early Roman artefacts from the 1st and 2nd centuries BC were found in the fill of several underground rock-cut chambers, either roofed cisterns or cellars which seem to date from the earliest Greco–Roman city on the site. The colonnaded South Decumanus, whose foundation has been dated to around AD 170, probably had rows of shops along both sides, but nothing of these remains today. No architectural remains have survived from the Byzantine period either. Most of the Roman and Byzantine structures were totally cleared away by the Umayyad inhabitants of the city, in the aftermath of a severe earthquake in the mid-7th century, in order to build the new housing area whose restored remains can be seen today.

Archaeological evidence dates the original Umayyad house to around 660 (perhaps part of a major rebuilding after the earthquake of 658). The original South Decumanus remained in use at this time, but its shops were totally rebuilt. The restored structure standing today was a single, large Umayyad house of at least ten rooms arranged east and west of a central courtyard. The courtyard was reached either by a passage between two shops along the *decumanus*, or by a back entrance staircase from the higher northern level. The irregular shape of the courtyard was dictated by the re-use of foundations inherited from the preceding periods. The floors of some of the rooms were covered with mosaics, traces of which have been found in a few places. It is thought, but not substantiated, that the house may have had a second storey entered directly from the higher northern ground, while it certainly had several basement rooms underground. A sewer drain winds its way underneath the courtyard in a north–south direction, and once emptied into the municipal sewerage system underneath the *decumanus*. The walls of the Umayyad house were uniformly made of re-used Romano–Byzantine stones filled in with stone chips and earth. The interior walls were probably mud-plastered, and the rooms were covered with wooden-beam roofs. Three pairs of rooms had inter-connecting doors forming two-room 'suites', a common feature of early Islamic urban housing. The entire house measured 13 metres from north to south and 21 metres from east to west, and had an interior surface area of about 200 square metres.

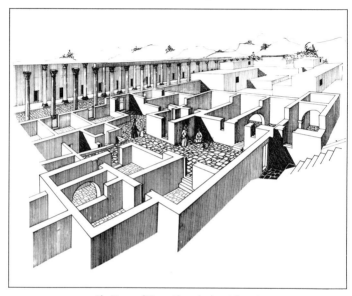

The Umayyad House (*drawn by Antoni Ostrasz*)

Around the middle of the 8th century, the large single house was partitioned into three smaller units, with much rebuilding of old walls and remodelling to open or block doors and form new rooms and passageways. The shops along the street were incorporated into the lower dwelling, which was entered through a courtyard fronting the street columns. Coin evidence shows three dwellings were used into the late 8th century, at least until 770. Massive stone tumble suggests the area was finally abandoned as a residential quarter after earthquake damage during the late 8th or early 9th-century Abbasid era. Four small stone-and-brick Abbasid pottery kilns were excavated among the ruins of the former house. Artefacts uncovered from the kiln areas included 9th-century Abbasid cooking pots, lamps, bowls and some green-glazed potsherds.

The Polish excavations here have contributed significantly to our understanding of life in Jerash during the Umayyad and early Abbasid years, clearly verifying that city life continued smoothly at Jerash through the Byzantine and Umayyad years. The many Umayyad lamps with Christian symbols on them (crosses, fish or inscriptions) also attest to the presence of an active Christian community during the Umayyad era. The work here has also documented more firmly the continued use of the city into the 9th-century Abbasid era, though urban life at this time would have been more modest than the city had been accustomed to in the previous eight hundred years.

GROUP 4

THE NYMPHAEUM

The Nymphaeum, a public fountain or water collection point dedicated to nymphs, is one of Jerash's smaller public monuments, but also one of the most finely decorated. It was built towards the very end of the 2nd century AD. With its richly carved niches, columns and statues, and the sound and sight of sparkling water softly splashing, it must have provided a delightful interlude for people strolling along the Cardo. The presence of the Nymphaeum along the Cardo is marked by two pairs of massive Corinthian columns that tower above the other columns of the street's western colonnade. Three of the four are original, while the one to the far left has been recently restored by the Department of Antiquities.

The 22-metre-wide Nymphaeum is built flush against the hillside, forming part of the retaining wall for the higher terraces to the west. The centre of the structure is a large, 11-metre-diameter semicircular recess flanked by two short walls. Seven alternately semicircular and rectangular niches adorn both the upper and lower stories of the recess, with flanking niches on the straight north and south walls. All the niches housed statues, and

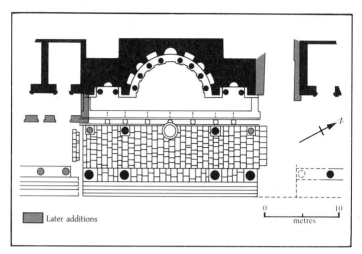

Later additions

0   10
metres

The Nymphaeum (*after C.S. Fisher*)

were flanked by small, free-standing Corinthian columns. The lower columns carried a richly carved entablature that broke forward and separated the two storeys, while the upper circular niches were topped by broken pediments. From a line just above these broken pediments, a half-dome rose to cover the entire recess. Beside the ornate stone carving, the lower storey of the Nymphaeum was covered in green Aegean marble, and the upper storey was plastered and richly painted. The inside of the half-dome was probably either gilded or painted.

Water passing through the statues of the lower storey emptied into a large basin that ran along the entire length of the Nymphaeum facade, and was enclosed on the street side by a low, straight and simply decorated wall. The wall was pierced by seven small channels that exited via lion heads on the sidewalk side of the basin, where passers-by could reach out and refresh themselves by touching the water. Six of the lion fountains emptied into low circular basins set in a small step below the wall; the third from the right retains its carved motif of four dolphins. The central channel emptied into the large red granite basin, the *laver*, that was added to the Nymphaeum later in the Byzantine period. The water finally trickled into an underground channel that carried it away from the fountain.

79

The Nymphaeum

The granite basin was flanked by two pairs of free-standing columns that align precisely with the four large Corinthian columns along the Cardo, and may once have carried statues. Scholars still debate whether a full roof projected from the inner recess to the four large Corinthian columns along the Cardo, or whether the Nymphaeum sported only the half-dome over the recess, as Browning suggests, thereby allowing sufficient light to strike the richly ornamented facade and bring it all to life.

Carving along the upper level of the Nymphaeum

THE UMAYYAD MOSQUE

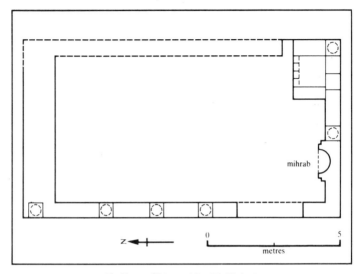

The Umayyad Mosque (*after Aida Naghwei*)

Walking north along the Cardo, about twenty-five metres past the Artemis Temple Propylaeum and just before the street is interrupted by the dirt service road, you will see four standing columns along the Cardo's eastern (right-hand side) colonnade. Climb up the four steps, pass through the columns, and walk forward (to the east) about ten metres, picking your way through assorted wall lines and fallen stones. You will reach an attractively paved room with a collection of column drums huddled together in the centre. These are the remains of the only 7th–8th-century Umayyad mosque discovered in Jerash to date. It was cleared and studied in 1981 by Mrs Aida Naghwei, the representative of the Jordanian Department of Antiquities in Jerash.

The mosque was built within the colonnaded *atrium* of an earlier Roman house. The mosque's central chamber measured 6.4 by 13.7 metres and was surrounded by columns that supported the roof; the column bases are best preserved today in the west wall. The *mihrab*, or prayer niche, in the south wall made use of an earlier Roman decorative niche. The *mihrab* remains

The Umayyad Mosque

standing today to a height of 1.55 metres. The main entrance to the mosque was in the west wall, with another in the south-eastern corner. The 2 by 1.3 metre raised platform in the south-east corner was probably used for preaching. In the north-west corner, several steps led up to a platform that may have been used to issue the call to prayer. A separate, 2.58-metre-square room south-west of the mosque had a water pipe connecting it with the Cardo. Another room east of the mosque was paved with mosaics and is thought to have been for the exclusive use of the *Imam*, the mosque's highest religious authority.

THE WEST BATHS

Just before reaching the North Tetrapylon, slightly below and to the right, you will see the sprawling, lonely ruins of one of the single largest structures of ancient Gerasa – the West Baths. Lying on a small terrace below the Cardo, but some 12 metres higher than the River Chrysorhoas, the West Baths once measured 75 metres in length by just over 50 metres in width; you have to walk through the ruins to appreciate their size. The building has never been excavated, but its plan was studied and sketched in the early decades of the century by Mr A. Harrison, an architect with the British mandate government in Palestine.

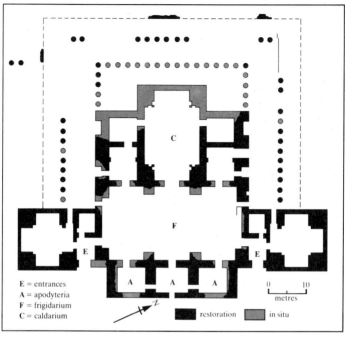

E = entrances
A = apodyteria
F = frigidarium
C = caldarium

0 ___ 10
metres

restoration   in situ

The West Baths (*after C.S. Fisher and A. St J. Harrison*)

The West Baths components reflect those of a typical Roman baths complex, with entrance area, changing rooms, cold bath, hot bath and adjacent dry area used for the socialising that was a key part of the ritual of Roman baths. The building is badly ruined now, cluttered with the fallen debris of its walls, columns, arches and domed roofs. But its plan can still be appreciated, particularly when viewed from the level of the Cardo. The large central structure included the two main entrances on the east, perhaps from a small side street that intersected with the North Decumanus. Three equal-sized rooms between the entrances were the *apodyteria*, or changing rooms. These led directly westwards into the huge, 35-metre-long central chamber that seems to have been the *frigidarium*, or cold bath, where bathers soaked gently in a large pool before moving on to the hot water rooms. The *frigidarium* was divided into three sections by large arches springing from piers on both sides of the room, all of which

The West Baths

was probably covered by a barrel-vaulted roof, according to a brief report on the baths in the Kraeling study of the early 1930s. Bathers passed through a large doorway in the western wall of the *frigidarium* into the 15-metre-square *caldarium*, or hot bath, with its walls full of heating flues that allowed the evacuation of gases from the furnace area somewhere around the perimeter of the baths. The square room had a large domed roof, and two similar recesses in its east and west walls. Two pairs of smaller rooms are located to its north and south, but their function is still unclear. The *caldarium* and these flanking rooms gave access to, and were surrounded from the north, west and south, by a U-shaped *peristyle*, or colonnaded courtyard.

A few tenacious columns on the north side of the *peristyle* can still be seen, defiantly standing guard. At the far north and south ends of the baths are two identical square pavilions, entered from the inside of the baths complex or from the external *peristyle*. The pavilions, which gave access to the roof of the baths, each had a fine domed roof supported by four arches. The northern one is still well preserved and is worth a close look. These hemispherical stone vaults over square rooms may be the earliest surviving examples of this architectural technique in the land of Syria.

This complex and the East Baths across the river were the city's two big public baths. They are the biggest such examples in Jordan and appear to be early Roman, probably dating from the 2nd century AD. The fine baths being excavated by a Danish team

Domed roof of the north pavilion of the West Baths

at Umm Qais (ancient Gadara) in north Jordan are another good example of Roman baths, but date from the later Byzantine period.

GROUP 5

THE NORTH TETRAPYLON

The North Tetrapylon, at the intersection of the Cardo and the North Decumanus, was not part of the original 1st-century town plan of the city. It was added sometime towards the end of the 2nd century AD, probably as part of the 'monumentalisation' of the entire quarter of the city around the North Theatre. The original Cardo colonnade, which once ran uninterrupted through the area of the *tetrapylon*, had several columns removed to make room for the new monument. The square *tetrapylon* had 5.5-metre-wide arches on all four sides, leading into a circular,

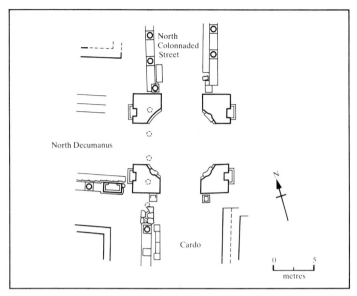

The North Tetrapylon (*after Warwick Ball*)

possibly domed, interior with plastered walls. Shallow pilasters flank the arches and the niches on the east and west faces, while free-standing columns flank the north and south archways. Lion-head fountains adorned the pedestals of the Corinthian columns on the north and south faces. The *tetrapylon* is typical of many other such structures found throughout the Roman Empire, usually commemorative arches located at the focal point of intersecting colonnaded streets. Examples include those at Palmyra, Ladikkiya and Philippopolis. A relief block depicting a moon-goddess found on the collapsed western facade of the *tetrapylon*, and another sun-god relief found on the collapsed eastern facade, may indicate the monument also served some religious function. The late 2nd-century date is ascertained in part by the carved decorative motif on the upper entablature, which is also found on other, well dated Roman buildings in Jordan such as the Qasr Nuweijis mausoleum near Amman and the Artemis Temple Propylaeum at Jerash. The North Tetrapylon was restored by Mr Warwick Ball.

THE NORTH COLONNADED STREET

The entire Cardo south of the North Tetrapylon was widened and adapted to the Corinthian order in the 2nd century AD. The North Colonnaded Street, however, retains the architectural charm and urban modesty of the earliest Roman town.

The North Colonnaded Street, looking towards the North Gate

Between the North Tetrapylon and the North Gate of the city, the North Colonnaded Street is the only remaining stretch of the original Cardo constructed in the 1st century AD. The Ionic order of the colonnade is broken only at one point (after the 16th column from the North Tetrapylon), where four slightly larger Corinthian columns probably mark the entrance to an unexcavated public building. Is this perhaps an eastern entrance to the same building or complex of buildings whose southern entrance is marked by the two Corinthian columns that interrupt the Ionic colonnade along the North Decumanus? Only future excavations will tell. In any case, this stretch of the North Colonnaded Street was restored many years ago, and its configuration today may or may not reflect the original layout in Roman days. Scattered pieces of yet more Corinthian capitals on the ground closer to the North Tetrapylon suggest there may have been another series of Corinthian columns interrupting the Ionic colonnade.

THE NORTH GATE

The North Gate, at the northernmost end of the Cardo, is one of the architecturally intriguing monuments of the city. Inscriptional evidence confirms it was built in AD 115, under the Legate of Trajan, C. Claudius Severus, who was responsible for rebuilding the road that left Jerash from this spot and probably travelled to Pella. Like the North-West Gate, it had a single passageway, 5.40 metres wide and 9.15 metres high as conjecturally restored. On each side of the north and south openings are two-storey bays each flanked by engaged Corinthian columns. Inscription panels, now illegible, rested on top of the archways.

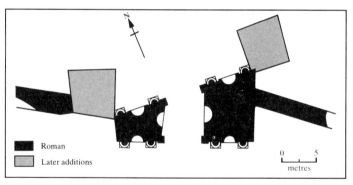

The North Gate (*after A.H. Detweiler*)

The 21.75-metre north face of the gate is 1.65 metres wider than the south face, with slightly wider bays. The two faces are not parallel to each other: the north face swings out at an eighteen-degree angle, giving the whole gate a wedge-shaped appearance. This allowed the gate's north passageway to line up squarely with the road from the north, while the south passageway lined up squarely with the Cardo inside the city walls. In effect, the line of the road from Pella turned the corner as it passed through the North Gate and met up with the Cardo, imitating similar 'out of line' architectural forms at Palmyra and Ephesus.

The existing structure seems to have been built near the foundations of an earlier gate, probably located some five metres to the south. The new North Gate demanded a rather awkward outward extension of the city walls, and the new wall sections, at 2.25 metres thick, are 75 centimetres narrower than the rest of the city wall. The two large, trapezoidal bastions on either side of the outer face of the North Gate were Byzantine or even later additions, and are only loosely connected to the gate. Also noteworthy are the gate's 7.7-metre-deep foundations, which include an elaborate underground water drainage system composed of roofed stone canals using moulded blocks from the older gate.

Mr A.H. Detweiler, who excavated the gate in the 1930s, noted that because of its awkward angles, elaborate foundations and provisions for drainage, it was probably 'the work of an engineer rather than an architect'.

THE NORTH THEATRE COMPLEX

Seventy metres to the west of the North Tetrapylon, the North Decumanus reaches the North Theatre complex, composed of the North Theatre itself and a 'plaza' in front of it. British, American and Australian teams jointly excavated many parts of the North Theatre area in 1982–3 as part of the Jerash International Project, and restoration work on the area continues today.

The 'plaza' in front of the theatre is something of an illusion, for the width of the North Decumanus does not, in fact, change when it reaches the theatre. Rather, the plaza effect was created by the presence along the north side of the street of a 12-metre-high Corinthian colonnade of six columns (five of which still stand) on the same line as the 6-metre-high Ionic colonnade along the rest of the street. On the south side of the *decumanus*, the street-level Ionic colonnade is interrupted, adding to the illusion of an open plaza in front of the theatre.

From the sidewalk, the main approach to the theatre was up a 14-metre-wide monumental staircase of 13 steps, broken by a landing. Two large niches, converted into fountains in the Byzantine era, flank the staircase, the one on the right as you go up the stairs being best preserved today. At the top of the

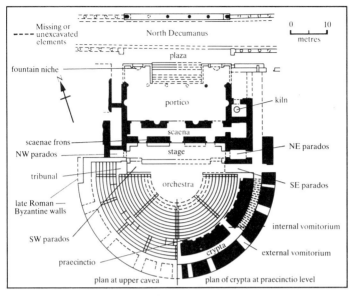

The North Theatre (*after John Stewart*)

staircase were four large, free-standing Corinthian columns that once formed the north end of the 10-metre-deep portico. Only the easternmost of these four columns remains standing today, to your left as you approach the theatre.

The theatre itself had two main phases during its lifetime. It was dedicated, and probably completed, in AD 164/65. It was an *odeon*, or small, probably covered, theatre or recital hall used for poetry readings, meetings or more modest performances than the large dramatic events that would have taken place in the city's larger South Theatre. The *odeon* may also have been the city council's meeting hall. It was modified several times and considerably enlarged in the first quarter of the 3rd century, and rededicated sometime during the period AD 222–35, according to inscriptional evidence. It finally went out of use as a theatre by the 5th to 6th centuries.

The original 2nd-century AD theatre included the existing portico, a 3.4-metre-thick *scaena* wall at the back of the stage, the existing 14 rows of seats of the lower *cavea*, or auditorium, two *paradoi*, or vaulted side passageways leading into the front of the

The North Theatre, seen from the north Plaza area

theatre, and five existing internal *vomitoria*, or arched passage-ways, leading in and out of the theatre from the top row of auditorium seats, passing at the top of the seats through the 2.7-metre-high wall decorated with niches. The auditorium was divided into four sections by five staircases that each led into one of the *vomitoria*. On some of the seats of the lower *cavea* are inscribed in Greek the names of the voting tribes (*phylai*) that were represented in the *boule*, or city council. Except for one tribe named after the Roman Emperor Hadrian, the others are named after Olympian gods. Most provincial Roman cities in the east had city councils that were composed typically of 50 representatives from each of 10–12 tribes, making for a city council of 500–600 members. The tribal names inscribed on the seats of the North Theatre, though not uncommon elsewhere in the Roman Empire, are the only ones of their kind yet found in the Middle East. According to Julian Bowsher, who was in charge of inscriptions during the 1982–3 excavations, this may verify that the theatre was also used as a *bouleterion*, or city council meeting-hall.

The theatre's expansion in the first quarter of the 3rd century AD included the addition of eight rows of seats that now form the upper *cavea*, doubling the theatre's capacity to around 1600 people. The top row of seats of the earlier lower *cavea* was transformed into a *praecinctio*, or a passageway that allowed

A Greek inscription on a seat of the North Theatre

spectators to move laterally between the lower and upper *caveae*. The upper *cavea* was supported by the archways of the internal *vomitoria* and the theatre's substantial, new external wall. At least four, and perhaps eight, external *vomitoria* pierced the external wall. Between the external and internal *vomitoria*, a large, vaulted internal corridor, the *crypta*, ran around the entire length of the theatre. The *crypta* is covered by a four-metre-high barrel vault springing from the walls. The three best preserved external *vomitoria*, at the western end of the upper auditorium, show their original construction of three independent, semicircular arches rising towards the exterior, with evidence of large wooden doors that could have been opened or closed to control access to the theatre. The semicircular external limestone wall of the theatre is currently visible to a height of 5.5 metres in the west, and over 10.5 metres in the north-east. Double, semicircular arches crown the *vomitoria* where they break through the external wall. Along the top of the theatre are the remains of six pairs of large (1.35 by 2.2 metres) rectangular assemblies which probably held in place a *velarium*, or awning, common to Roman theatres. Ten shallow post holes in the lower and upper *cavea* seats may have held posts which helped open and close the awning. At the far western end of the *praecinctio*, within the *vomitorium*, can be seen the well preserved small staircase that the audience climbed to reach the top rows of seats.

When the theatre was expanded in the early 3rd century AD, the stage area also underwent extensive remodelling, according to the archaeologists who excavated it and the 1982–3 architectural studies of John D. Stewart and Susan Balderstone.

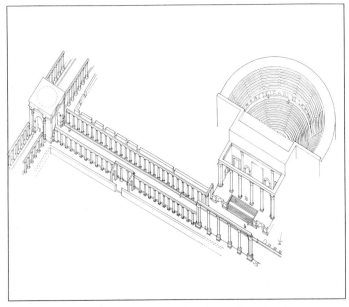

The North Theatre, North Decumanus and North Tetrapylon in the 3rd
century AD, preliminary hypothetical reconstruction. The extent of roofing and
the design of neighbouring buildings are uncertain (*drawn by John Stewart*)

The original *scaena* wall, facing the audience from behind the
stage, was dismantled and replaced by a more complex *scaena*
composed of two parallel walls. The 1.72-metre-thick internal
wall, or *scaenae frons*, was dismantled and rebuilt in a slightly more
forward position, closer to the audience. Behind it was a 2.15-
metre-wide corridor, separating it from the 1.75-metre-thick
external *scaena* facade that faced the outside portico, plaza and the
North Decumanus. The two walls of the *scaena* structure almost
certainly reached a height of 16 metres, to correspond to the full
height of the top rows of the upper auditorium. The elaborate
scaenae frons was probably two storeys high, and was adorned
with coloured marble, free-standing Corinthian columns and
broken entablatures, behind which were semicircular niches
decorated with mosaics. In front of this, the 5-metre-deep stage
was probably covered with wooden planks carried on beams
inserted into sockets in the foundation walls of the *scaenae frons* or

supported from below by posts. East and west of the stage area four *paradoi*, or covered passageways, provided access to the theatre from the north, to both the orchestra and stage levels. Only the two, arched western *paradoi* entrances are well preserved today. Directly above the orchestra *paradoi* on both sides were the *tribunalia*, or the tribunals that were reserved for dignitaries and sponsors of events that took place in the theatre. The tribunals had more elaborate seats whose remains were found in the rubble during excavations. White limestone statues decorated the interior of the theatre, along with some white limestone herms, life-sized representations of an idealized Greek youth's head with a stylized, tapered shaft. The 2nd-century AD Roman herms from Jerash were copies of 4th-century BC Greek types.

By the mid-3rd century AD, the theatre seems to have started losing some of its special status as a major public building, for urban development to the north-west began encroaching upon it. Several Roman and Byzantine walls have been excavated against the north-west external wall of the theatre. In the 6th century, the construction of the adjacent Church of Bishop Isaiah completed the transformation of the area. The entire theatre building seems to have gone out of use as a theatre by the 5th century. It was badly damaged in an earthquake in the middle of the 6th century, perhaps AD 551, which caused the collapse of the *scaena* walls and some of the upper rows of auditorium seats. The ruins provided conveniently cut stones that were re-used by the Byzantine inhabitants of the city to build other structures. In the 7th and early 8th century, the sad wreck of the former theatre was turned into an industrial complex for pottery production. A series of kilns was built among and on top of the collapsed stones of the former theatre. Some simple rooms and small houses were built within the protective walls of the still standing internal vaults and passages, or against the external south wall. Such 'squatter' occupation seems to have continued, in various degrees, until the 14th–16th centuries in the *crypta* and the west *parados* of the orchestra area.

Initial planning for the restoration of the theatre, and consolidation work, was done by John D. Stewart. Since 1985, reconstruction work has been done by a Department of Antiquities team headed by Professor H. Kalayan.

THE UMAYYAD KILNS

The series of 7th–8th-century Umayyad kilns built into different parts of the ruins of the former theatre was excavated and studied in 1982–4 by British and American archaeologists. In all, eight Umayyad kilns were excavated in Jerash in this period, five of which were in the North Theatre area. They are particularly valuable because they are the only such Umayyad kilns ever documented in Jordan to date, though other excavated kilns may have been Umayyad but not recognised as such. Dr Jerome Schaefer and Mr Robin Falkner excavated the theatre kilns, and noted two main types:

(a) a reduction kiln, which was blocked during the last stages of firing to prevent oxygen from entering, producing characteristically grey-coloured basins, bowls, jars and tiles;

(b) an oxidation kiln, which remained open to the air during firing, produced red or brown-coloured cooking pots, casseroles, jars, bowls, pitchers and lamps.

The most interesting ones were typically up to 2.5 metres high, cylindrical, domed brick updraft kilns with an external firebox, an internal lower chamber through which the heat passed, and an internal upper firing chamber. They were probably fuelled by dung, twigs, finely split wood and charcoal. The internal firing chamber was supported by a central platform made of a mud-brick shell filled with rubble. The early 8th-century pottery from the Jerash kilns is almost identical to pottery excavated at Pella, Amman and other nearby areas where no Umayyad kilns have ever been found. With the discovery since the 1930s of at least fourteen other Umayyad or Byzantine kilns at Jerash, this brings up the possibility that early 8th-century Jerash was an important regional centre for the ceramics industry which exported its production to nearby cities.

THE NORTH DECUMANUS

The stretch of the North Decumanus between the North Tetrapylon and the North Theatre Plaza was excavated for the first time in 1982–3 by an Australian team under the direction of Mr Alan Walmsley. The 9.2-metre-wide North Decumanus, well paved with regularly laid limestone slabs, is flanked by 4.25-

metre-wide sidewalks bordered by walls with 4.5-metre-deep foundation trenches to the north and south. A drain of ceramic pipes below the north sidewalk fed the lion's-head fountains in the North Tetrapylon. The street surface is bowed up slightly to allow water to run off. Longer slabs in the middle of the street cover an underground drain that is pierced at 14-metre intervals by stone man-hole covers with the remains of cemented iron lifting rings.

The colonnades on both sides of the street are of the Ionic order, except for two restored Corinthian columns and two piers on the north side that probably mark the entrance to an important public building built at a later date. The Ionic columns seem to have been re-used from the colonnade that flanked the old Cardo, before it was widened. Archaeologist Warwick Ball of Australia, who has studied the street, notes that none of the North Decumanus column bases and drums fit exactly on top of one another, indicating a clear re-use.

Archaeological and architectural studies suggest the original North Decumanus was laid out in the late 1st century AD. The south wall of the street was pierced by eight doorways that probably led into shops, while the north wall was originally unbroken. The street was apparently colonnaded and repaved at the end of the 2nd century, some time after 165, when the whole area was 'monumentalised' to fit into the new architectural scheme that included the construction of the North Theatre, the North Plaza and the North Tetrapylon. The Decumanus east of the North Tetrapylon remained unpaved and without columns. In the early 3rd century, perhaps when the theatre was expanded around AD 230, the south wall near the theatre was dismantled to make way for a 9.15-metre-wide monumental staircase that may have been linked with the theatre expansion. Some years later, a major public building was constructed behind the north wall, entered through a 3.2-metre-wide doorway behind the two standing Corinthian columns.

By the early 5th century, the entrances through the north and south walls had been blocked, indicating either that the rooms behind them had fallen out of use or that the street entrances were blocked and the rooms were entered through other doors. This is the case in the rooms excavated by Pam Watson along the south intersection of the North Decumanus and the Cardo, in which the door from the North Decumanus had been blocked; the room was still used but was entered through doors along the Cardo. Most of the North Decumanus columns and sidewalk paving stones were removed in the 6th century, when some of the columns seem to have been re-used in the construction of the nearby Church of Bishop Isaiah.

British and American archaeologists of the Jerash International Project dug several test trenches in 1983 in the area between the North Theatre and the North-West Gate of the city, hoping to ascertain whether or not the North Decumanus continued on a straight line to the North-West Gate. One trench was sunk between the tops of two columns projecting from the earth at a point some 150 metres east of the gate, on the assumption that it might intersect with the line of the North Decumanus. No trace of the street was encountered, suggesting either that the North Decumanus did not run in a straight line from the North Tetrapylon to the North-West Gate, or perhaps that the street was never completed in this north-western quarter of the city. The excavators encountered several walls associated with 6th–7th-century AD soil layers. An earlier foundation wall built on bed-rock seems to be associated with 4th–5th-century AD occupation levels.

In the northern part of the trench, two columns still *in situ* stood in front of a well constructed ashlar wall, built into bed-rock and running in an east–west direction. Another wall, running in a north–south direction, abutted the westernmost column. The excavators have suggested tentatively that these two columns may belong to the south side of the North Decumanus, which may have diverged slightly to the north at this point on its way to the North-West Gate.

Another trench, sunk sixty metres south of the North-West Gate, came down upon two stone walls, collapsed stones and a fragmentary plaster surface, with associated pottery, coins and other artefacts dating from the 3rd–4th centuries AD. This area seems to have been occupied mainly in the 3rd century, but the precise nature and extent of the Roman presence in this part of the city must await further excavation.

The North-West Gate itself was completed in AD 75–6 according to an inscription recovered from the collapsed lintel.

Unlike the north and south gates of the city, it was never subsequently redesigned or rebuilt, and today it is simply a mass of tumbled stones protruding slightly above the line of the city walls.

THE CHURCH OF BISHOP ISAIAH

On a terrace overlooking the North Theatre from the west is the Church of Bishop Isaiah, discovered and excavated by the American team under the direction of Dr Vincent Clark during the 1982-3 work of the Jerash International Project. The triple-apsed basilical church measures 28 metres by 18 metres, and is best preserved to a height of two metres in its south-west corner. It is composed of an 8.3-metre-wide central nave and two side aisles ending in internal apses, with colonnades separating the nave from the side aisles. A large chancel area was separated from the rest of the church by a chancel screen set on a single step. A portico along the entire west side of the church was formed by a stylobate of eight columns.

The Church of Bishop Isaiah

The main apse was surrounded by two rows of seats with a raised, projecting throne in the rear for the bishop. The floor of the entire church, except for the stone-paved apses, is covered with rich mosaics that include geometric patterns, alternating diamonds and squares, portraits of donors, inscriptions, grape-vines, birds, fruit trees, gazelles, deer, peacocks, plants, flowers and humans. The mosaics have been reburied for protection.

The church was almost certainly built in 559, placing it chronologically between the Church of SS Peter and Paul (540) and the Church of Bishop Genesius (611). It was used as a church for almost 200 years, and appears to have been abandoned in the mid-8th century after an earthquake, perhaps the big earthquake of 747. It seems to have been undergoing repairs to the roof and walls when it was abandoned, to judge by plaster patches along the floor and twenty-four roof tiles that were stacked in the south aisle, next to many basins, bowls and jugs that were used to mix and carry fresh plaster. It was re-used briefly in the Mamluke era, as was the adjacent North Theatre, when the north chancel area and the apse were cleared and re-used as a room. It was abandoned again from the 15th century until its rediscovery in 1982.

The church had nine doors when first built, three each on its north, west and south sides, though all but two were blocked up when it finally went out of use. It was used throughout most of the Umayyad era, but like most other churches in the area almost all its mosaics of human and animal figures were defaced during the iconoclastic reign of the Umayyad Caliph Yazid II (720–4).

Most of the pottery from the church was typical late Umayyad ware, from the first half of the 8th century. Eighteen datable coins were found, along with many iron nails, spikes and fastenings, and typical pale blue and blue-green Byzantine and late Umayyad glass fragments, mostly from lamp stems, bowls, goblets and window glass. Fifteen new inscriptions were discovered. The most important was a large mosaic inscription in front of the central apse, giving the name of Bishop Isaiah of Jerash and the date of the church's construction.

GROUP 6

THE TEMPLE OF ARTEMIS COMPLEX

The Temple of Artemis, dedicated to the patron goddess of the city, was the single most important monument of ancient Jerash.

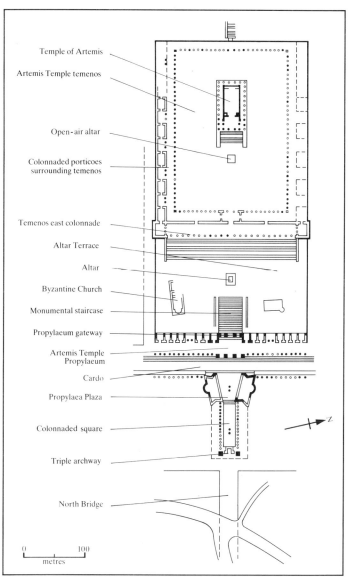

Temple of Artemis

Artemis Temple temenos

Open-air altar

Colonnaded porticoes
surrounding temenos

Temenos east colonnade

Altar Terrace

Altar

Byzantine Church

Monumental staircase

Propylaeum gateway

Artemis Temple
Propylaeum

Cardo

Propylaea Plaza

Colonnaded square

Triple archway

North Bridge

0   100
metres

The Artemis Temple complex during the 2nd century AD (*after R. Parapetti*)

This is reflected in its size (only the Hippodrome is larger), and in the architectural complexity of the temple compound and its elaborate approach up a Sacred Way that started on the east bank of the river. It is situated such that it is visible from almost every corner of the city, particularly when one first enters the city from the north or south gates. The temple complex was first studied in detail by C.S. Fisher in the 1930s, and is being examined by the Italian Archaeological Expedition in Jerash under the field direction of Dr Roberto Parapetti, which forms part of the Jerash International Project.

Most visitors today approach the temple from along the Cardo. Walking north along the Cardo, just beyond the Nymphaeum you will see, to the left, the standing remains of four enormous Corinthian columns; to the right, a series of large carved stones lined up along the pavement of the Cardo. Just in front of the four columns, turn to the right, walk up four steps and down another four; this will bring you into an area full of tumbled stones and columns in the midst of wild vegetation and a nicely paved small plaza. Walk straight ahead (east) about twenty-five metres until you reach a series of seven Corinthian columns on your right. Straight in front of you the path will be blocked by the semicircular apse of a Byzantine church. Turn around and face the Artemis Temple (to the west), which you can see high up in the distance. You are now in a position to start walking up the Sacred Way that led to the temple.

The Sacred Way started behind you, on the east bank of the city, and crossed the river on the **North Bridge**. Only the west abutment of the bridge remains today, on the left-hand side of the main road through the modern city as you drive north. The bridge is slightly off the axis of the temple and the Sacred Way, it has been suggested, in order to connect with a previous road on the east bank of the city. At the end of the bridge on the west bank of the city, a monumental staircase once led up into a triple archway that in turn opened into a long, colonnaded square, or street, inclined slightly uphill to the west. The seven columns standing today once formed the southern colonnade of this square or street. The 38-metre-long, 11-metre-wide square ended at the west in a small staircase that entered the **Propylaeum Plaza**; this in turn opened onto the Cardo. The colonnaded square and the Propylaeum Plaza appear rather forlorn today, and somewhat confusing to the modern visitor. This is because of the chaotic, abandoned state of the ruins, and the fact that the original 2nd-century AD Roman structures were changed considerably during the 6th-century Byzantine period.

The Propylaeum Plaza was a unique, butterfly-shaped trapezium, eleven metres wide on the east but nineteen metres wide on the west where it opened onto the Cardo. The flared internal walls of the Plaza accommodated fountains, while large pillars flanked the internal passageways and the east and west ends of the Plaza. The north and south walls of the Plaza were interrupted in their centre by an open, semicircular recess flanked by two columns. The purpose of the peculiar shape of the Plaza, according to Dr Parapetti, was 'to create a dynamic expanding space able to visually overcome the gap created by the Cardo which separates the square from the (temple) propylaeum opposite'.

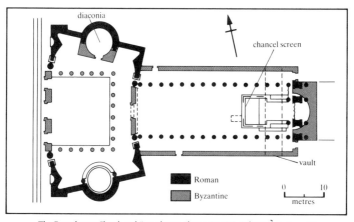

The Propylaeum Church and Propylaeum Plaza (*after C.S. Fisher and R. Parapetti*)

The original 2nd-century AD colonnaded square, or street, was transformed into a Byzantine church in the 6th century. This has been dubbed the **Propylaeum Church**, because of its location in the *propylaeum*, the stately entrance to the temple precinct. Sometime in the second half of the 6th century, after earthquakes destroyed much of the colonnaded square, the triple archway and the North Bridge, the Byzantine inhabitants of the

The Propylaeum Church

city cleverly transformed the square into a basilical church. The triple archway at the eastern end of the square was largely removed and replaced by the semicircular apse of the church that remains today. The western end of the square was blocked off by a new wall, and the entire area of the former square was roofed. The new church's nave was formed by the two rows of the former square's columns, with side aisles on either side of the colonnades. Inside the former Propylaeum Plaza was built the new church's atrium, an open-air courtyard surrounded by columns. The semicircular recess in the north wall of the Plaza was expanded into a circular room with a fine mosaic floor dating from 565. It was part of the church complex, and served perhaps to receive offerings or to distribute charity to the poor.

From the Propylaeum Plaza, the Sacred Way crossed the Cardo and started its approach to the temple via a series of terraces and staircases. Five steps up from the Cardo to the west, the four huge Corinthian columns mark the front of the **Temple of Artemis Propylaeum**. The columns measure 1.42 metres in diameter and once stood 16 metres high. On either side of these columns were thirteen smaller columns, together marking off the 120-metre-long eastern side of the temple precinct. Flanking the Artemis Temple Propylaeum on both sides were rows of seven two-storey shops. The lower shops measured 5.3 by 5.9 metres each, and were entered from the sidewalk level; the upper shops, with pilaster-flanked windows overlooking the street, were reached by narrow staircases at the rear of the lower rooms.

Beyond the four large Corinthian columns, you pass into the 19.5 by 14.8-metre portico. The large carved stones lined up along the Cardo once formed the decorative elements carried above the portico, and were supported from the front by the four large Corinthian columns along the Cardo. A gentle staircase of ten steps separated by a small landing takes you from the portico, up through four smaller, free-standing Corinthian columns, to the monumental triple-gateway of the Propylaeum. The gateway, set back in a recess, is 2.15 metres thick, with a main central passageway that measured 5 metres wide and nearly 9 metres high. The smaller side doors were crowned by shallow niches flanked by corner pilasters. The entire upper level of the gateway was an elaborately carved ensemble of rich floral motifs, best preserved today above the northern side of the gateway, to your right as you face it. From the gateway, you can see the Temple of Artemis columns today, but in antiquity this view of the temple would have been blocked by the east *temenos* wall. After passing through the Propylaeum gateway, you walk up a monumental staircase composed of seven flights, each of seven steps and enclosed by high walls. At the top of this staircase you reach the **Altar Terrace**, with the foundation of the open-air altar in the centre. The Altar Terrace once formed a U-shape around the staircase from the Propylaeum gateway, and may have been framed by colonnaded porticoes. The terrace is fourteen metres above the level of the Cardo, and is supported from the east by the retaining wall that also forms the back wall of the row of two-storey shops along the Cardo.

From the Altar Terrace, a monumental staircase composed of three flights of nine steps each takes you up another seven metres to reach the level of the **Artemis Temple Temenos**, the sacred enclosure immediately surrounding the temple. This staircase was 105 metres wide, and spanned the full width of the Altar Terrace. At the top of the steps, you reach the *temenos* east

The Altar Terrace on the Sacred Way, with remains of the open-air altar in the foreground and the Artemis Temple in the background

colonnade, composed of a row of twenty-two Corinthian columns, of which eight have been partly restored (to your left as you reach the top of the stairs). Corner towers probably flanked the north and south extremities of the *temenos* east side. Some ten metres beyond this colonnade are the scanty remains of a doorway and, beyond that, the *temenos* proper. This was an open-air, rectangular area measuring 161 metres deep by 121 metres wide, surrounded on all four sides by colonnades that are best preserved today on the south side of the temple (to your far left). If you walk over to the southern side of the *temenos*, you can see the double row of columns that formed the colonnades around the *temenos*. The north and south colonnades each had 36 columns, the east and west colonnades 26 columns each, with square piers at the four corners. The north and south colonnades were deepened by alternating rooms and *exedrae*, or open, rectangular recesses between the columns.

About twenty metres directly in front of the temple, is a series of partly excavated walls and a well preserved arch. Next to the arch are the recently excavated, pink-coloured base stones of the original, 2nd-century AD open-air altar that stood in front of the temple. The arch and the walls themselves are the remains of a late Byzantine–Umayyad ceramics complex that was built on the site of the abandoned temple area. Pottery excavated here was all from the 7th and 8th centuries. As you approach the temple and stand at the foot of the steps, you will see to your right and left the remains of 7th or 8th-century Umayyad rooms that were related to the ceramics complex. Underneath these are the foundations of the original 2nd-century AD staircase that led up to the temple.

The Temple of Artemis

The **Temple of Artemis** itself, as C.S. Fisher wrote in the 1930s, was 'in all probability the finest single structure ever erected at ancient Gerasa'. It stood on a podium 22.6 metres wide and 40.1 metres long, with two side walls that projected 13.75 metres east of the temple to flank the central staircase. The original staircase was composed of two or three flights of steps interrupted by landings. A small modern staircase has been provided for the convenience of visitors. The solid inner and outer foundation walls supporting the temple vary in thickness from 2.4 to 7 metres. Between the foundation walls was a series of interconnecting, barrel-vaulted rooms and passageways entered through internal doorways at the south and north-east of the temple. Coming up into the temple, you can look down through four large stones surrounding a modern hole in the floor, through which can be seen the underground vaults which were probably used for storage. You can also enter the vaults through a door in the south wall of the main temple, though this too is a modern entrance that did not exist in antiquity. The north and south sides of the temple had eleven 13-metre-high columns, with six each on the shorter east and west sides. The portico at the very front of the temple had three rows of columns, each 1.5 metres thick and just over 13 metres high. All but one of the original twelve columns still stand in the temple portico.

The *cella* of the Temple of Artemis, looking west

From the portico, you walk up into the *cella*, or central chamber of the temple. The main entrance was through a 4.96-metre-wide, 9-metre-high doorway flanked by two niches in the 3.3-metre-deep front wall. The *cella* measures 13.37 by 24.15 metres. Its north, south and west walls were decorated on the outside with corner pilasters and on the inside with shallow, rectangular niches. The interior walls of the *cella* were covered throughout with thin marble slabs that were attached to the walls by hooks. The walls are dotted with the holes into which these hooks fitted. About halfway into the *cella*, two steps originally led up half a metre to a new level, from where a short staircase led to a large recess in the western wall. This 3.95 by 2.05-metre recess is some two metres higher than the level of the entrance of the *cella*, and faces you as you first step into the temple. It is spanned by two superimposed arches, and flanked by two small doors, all of which can be clearly seen today. This was the important spot where the shrine of the temple was located; it held the sacred cult-image of the goddess Artemis, the daughter of Zeus, sister of

Apollo and city-goddess of Roman Gerasa.

The exisiting temple has not been conclusively dated by inscriptional evidence, but is thought to date from the 2nd century AD, when the city was enjoying a period of prosperity and architectural glory. There is some architectural evidence to suggest the temple was never actually completed or used. The most noteworthy aspect of the Artemis Temple complex is not the temple building itself, but rather the 'spatial unfolding of the entire complex of buildings', in Dr Parapetti's words. Each monument or area within the entire complex – from the North Bridge to the Temple of Artemis – is a self-contained entity, but all are linked together in an organic, flowing whole. The approach along the Sacred Way from the bridge to the temple rises along several successive levels, at each point offering a vista towards the ultimate destination of the great temple itself. Dr Parapetti says that 'such a remarkable organic urban achievement (dating from the 2nd century AD) belongs to and is the expression of a new Eastern architectural school, to which we are indebted for the last inventions of the ancient world'.

Archaeological research by the Italian team continues around the Temple of Artemis. The area in front of the temple was re-used extensively in the Byzantine and Umayyad periods, mainly for pottery making. A series of Byzantine–Umayyad kilns has been excavated directly in front of the temple. In the 6th century AD, the Byzantine Gerasenes re-used the wider *temenos* area for religious purposes, and built a church on a filling three metres above the level of the Altar Terrace, south of the large staircase that connected the Artemis Temple *temenos* with the Altar Terrace. Its scanty remains can be seen today about fifteen metres south of the small weather station, reached by a well worn path from the south side of the Altar Terrace. The Arab inhabitants of Jerash also re-used the Artemis Temple building itself. They partly rebuilt some outside walls to transform it into a fortress that was captured and severely damaged in the 12th century by the forces of the Crusader King Baldwin II.

GROUP 7

THE CATHEDRAL GATE AND STAIRCASE

Just over a hundred metres north of the South Tetrakionion, the sidewalk along the left-hand side of the Cardo suddenly narrows, and is linked to the street by a long staircase composed of just three steps. At the top of these steps, eight Corinthian columns on square pedestals rise slightly higher than the rest of the Cardo colonnade, marking the presence of another important Roman public building behind them. This is believed to have been the original, 2nd-century AD Temple of Dionysus, reached through the elaborate doorway and staircase framed by the eight large Corinthian columns. The existing doorway, today called the Cathedral Gate, is a 4th-century AD rebuilding of the original *propylaeum*, or stately entrance, of the Temple of Dionysus. In the 4th century, with the advent of Christianity, certain pagan Roman temples throughout the eastern provinces of the Roman Empire were transformed into churches. In this case, the former *propylaeum* of the Roman Temple was slightly altered and reconstructed to form the impressive pavement-level entrance to the Cathedral and an associated complex of important buildings from the Christian period of the city.

Immediately behind the eight large Corinthian columns is a wall pierced by several doorways. This is a later 5th–6th-century Byzantine wall that formed the front of a row of shops. Immediately behind these rooms is another wall, the front of the original Roman shops that ran along the front of the Cardo, between the Cathedral Gate and the Nymphaeum. Mr J.W. Crowfoot, who excavated the area in 1929, collected bagfuls of charcoal from two of the earliest Roman rooms; the rooms had ceased to function as shops, and were transformed at some point into a blacksmith's workshop, with an anvil in one room and a charcoal store in the other. Another room with two unfinished stone capitals may have been a stone-mason's workshop. There is good evidence to indicate that the shops were two storeys high.

A small flight of five steps leads up to the threshold of the Cathedral Gate itself, flanked by two columns standing on pedestals. The gate's very fine stone carving is re-used and is

The Cathedral Gateway

among the city's best preserved artisanship from the second half of the 2nd century AD. The long staircase and enclosing walls inside the gate are not a 2nd-century AD Roman original; they are a 4th-century Byzantine rebuilding of the earlier Roman staircase that had a slightly gentler gradient. The four Corinthian columns immediately inside the gateway have their bases at different levels, but their capitals at the same level. On either side of the four columns are the remains of two small, unimpressive staircases. These are later, perhaps 7th-century, staircases leading up to the rooms above the street-front shops. The top of the flanking walls on both sides of the main staircase supported a colonnade of Ionic columns carrying a stepped architrave. This U-shaped colonnade went right around the staircase, carried over the top of the main gateway by a 'bridge' supported by the four Corinthian columns at the base of the staircase. The top of the staircase was spanned by a great arch, decorated with crosses.

THE SHRINE OF ST MARY

Worshippers arriving at the top of the staircase would have faced the outside eastern wall of the Cathedral, whose entrances they reached by walking along either of the two covered passages on the north and south sides of the Cathedral. But they would not have faced a bare wall at the top of the Cathedral Gate staircase. Facing them was the Shrine of St Mary, built against the eastern external face of the Cathedral from re-used, probably early 2nd-century AD, stone blocks. This was a rather simple structure, centred on a delicately carved shell-headed niche flanked by small pilasters. (See illustration on page 41.) Beneath the shell, the names 'Michael, Holy Mary, Gabriel' were painted in red letters; further traces of red-painted figures below them were possibly the faint remains of a red-gilded background. A metal plug in the centre may have held a lamp, and other plugs probably held a grille in place. This shrine has been dated by Crowfoot to no earlier than the second quarter of the 5th century, when, he notes, the cult of the Virgin Mary was becoming increasingly popular, and the two Archangels honoured here, Michael and Gabriel, were frequently mentioned together as the guardians of church entrances, doorways or towers. The rough block paving in front of the shrine was probably the foundation for a finer upper pavement, perhaps of marble, that was subsequently plundered. Below this paving, the 1929 excavators found the remains of several steps from the 2nd-century AD staircase; this led from the Cardo to the Roman Temple of Dionysus which they suggest was located here before the Cathedral was built.

THE CATHEDRAL

From the north and south sides of the Shrine of St Mary, paved passages whose roofs were carried on a series of arches led to the main, western entrance of the Cathedral. The wider eastern end of the north passage, or north *narthex*, may have been for use by women; the south *narthex*, blocked to the west by the wall of the later chapel, was for men, Kraeling suggests. The Cathedral had three main doors in its western wall, leading from the external *atrium* into a central nave and two side aisles. Four doors once pierced both the north and south walls of the building, with two more doors entering small rooms on either side of the apse. The central nave was separated from the side aisles by rows of twelve Corinthian columns that were re-used from an earlier, 2nd-century AD building, fragments of which can still be seen. At a

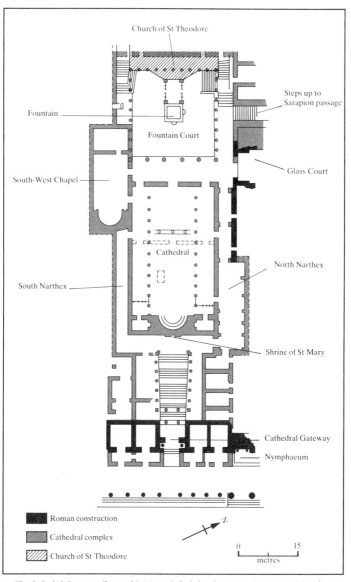

Church of St Theodore

Fountain

Steps up to Sarapion passage

Fountain Court

Glass Court

South-West Chapel

North Narthex

Cathedral

South Narthex

Shrine of St Mary

Cathedral Gateway

Nymphaeum

Roman construction

Cathedral complex

Church of St Theodore

0   15
metres

The Cathedral Gateway, Shrine of St Mary, Cathedral and Fountain Court (*after C.S. Fisher*) point four bays west of the apse, a chancel screen across the width of the nave marked off the chancel and altar area. Immediately south of the chancel screen was the *ambo*, or pulpit, alongside of which are the few remaining traces of the original paving of the nave. The pink limestone paving stones in the aisles, however, are largely intact. Seats for the clergy ran around the apse, with benches along the outer walls of the aisles.

The Cathedral

The Cathedral suffered severe structural damage during its lifetime. It was poorly rebuilt and simultaneously made smaller by constructing a wall across the nave and aisles at the point of the fifth column from the west, outside of which a three-column portico was erected. This portico rested directly on top of the foundations of the older west wall of the pagan Roman temple that stood on the site before the Cathedral was built.

The exact date of the Cathedral is unknown, due to a lack of inscriptions; indeed, the very function of the building as the Cathedral of Gerasa is not fully confirmed. Kraeling says 'this was once the most splendidly appointed church in Gerasa', full of marble, glass, coloured stone, mosaics and other decorative elements. It was also the city's earliest, and perhaps its most important, Christian church because of the special position it occupied in the centre of the city. It dates most likely from the second half of the 4th century, perhaps, as Kraeling deduces, from around 365.

Sometime during the second quarter of the 6th century the small **South-West Chapel** was added to the corner of the Cathedral. It blocked the west end of the Cathedral's south *narthex*, and also encroached upon the south-eastern corner of the colonnade of the adjacent Fountain Court. The chapel was not as well built as the Cathedral itself, with which it communicated through a small, poorly made door. Two other doors led into the east and south porticoes of the Fountain Court. The simple chapel had an apse flanked by two side-apses and separated by a chancel screen from the mosaic-covered nave. A small, simple *atrium* west of the chapel also took up part of the south portico of the Fountain Court.

THE FOUNTAIN COURT

Immediately west of the Cathedral is its *atrium*, now called the Fountain Court, probably built at the same time as the Cathedral. A fountain with miraculous associations stood in the centre of the square, colonnaded courtyard. Six re-used, late 2nd-century AD Corinthian columns stood on the east side of the *atrium*, forming the porticoed entrance to the Cathedral. The three other sides of the *atrium* had shorter, Ionic columns, but the entire west colonnade was removed to make space for the Church of St Theodore to the west; the columns of the south-east corner were removed in the 6th century to make room for the small chapel in the south-western corner of the Cathedral. The pavement under the eastern portico was divided into six panels, paved with red octagons and white squares that still exist, while the three other porticoes of the atrium seem to have been covered with mosaics. The courtyard in the middle was paved with rectangular stones.

The square fountain itself was built of pink limestone on three sides; re-used ceiling coffers on the west side may reflect a later rebuilding connected to the Church of St Theodore. For, when the church was built, its outer apse wall was connected to the

114

The Fountain Court, with the fountain in the foreground and the Church of
St Theodore in the background

west face of the fountain by two arches supporting a vault. A vault also covered the fountain itself, which had two basins attached to its north and east walls. The fountain was supplied with water from Birketein via a long conduit that skirted the eastern side of the Artemis Temple terrace and branched off at one point to supply the Nymphaeum as well. Water reached the fountain through a lead pipe buried beneath the existing line of obliquely laid paving stones running in a north-easterly direction from the fountain.

The fountain was probably the site of the annual Feast of the Miracle of Cana, when water was turned into wine. The Roman historian Epiphanius wrote in AD 375 that this feast took place every year at a fountain in Gerasa ('our brethren have drunk from the fountain in Gerasa which is in the martyrium . . .'). Some scholars believe that the city's early Christians may have adopted this ritual from an earlier pagan miracle that took place at the Temple of Dionysus in Jerash.

THE GLASS COURT

Directly north of the Cathedral and the Fountain Court are the ruins of two unexcavated classical buildings separated by a small court known today as the Glass Court. Located immediately north of the Corinthian portico between the Fountain Court and the Cathedral, the court's original floor level was 1.25 metres below the Cathedral floor. The original Roman court probably once led into the north portico of the Fountain Court. It was remodelled slightly at the time the Cathedral was built in the second half of the 4th century, when its function must have been associated with the Cathedral itself. Its floor was then also covered with eight panels of striking mosaics that have been studied but reburied under the earth for safe keeping. Sometime later (Kraeling suggests perhaps in the early 6th century), the floor level was raised to that of the Fountain Court, and a new mosaic floor laid, decorated with animals, vines and an acanthus scroll border. At a yet later date, the ruined room became part of a glass-making complex. It yielded over 120 lbs of different coloured melted glass chunks during excavations in the early 1930s, after which it was named the Glass Court.

THE SARAPION PASSAGE

To the left of the Glass Court, as you face it, and lining up directly with the fountain, is a fine staircase leading up to a triple doorway. This is the Sarapion Passage, named after an inscription from AD 67, found here in the 1930s. It mentions a certain Sarapion, son of Apollonius, who financed the construction of an *andron* for the Temple of Artemis (the precise function of an *andron* remains unknown, though it is thought to be some sort of passage). The triple doorway, at the top of the steps from the north portico of the Fountain Court, led into a room; this in turn opened on to a small street which ran between the south side of the Temple of Artemis complex and the Nymphaeum. The two flanking openings on either side of the main door are thought to have led to the roof above the north portico of the Fountain Court, from where spectators would have had a fine view of the ceremonies around the miraculous fountain.

THE STEPPED STREET

Turn left at the top of the Sarapion Passage and you will be facing the Stepped Street, so named because of the steps that interrupt

The Stepped Street

its natural slope. It now has an almost comic appearance because of the different angles of the wide steps that have endured so many centuries of human use and natural abuse. The street followed the path of a natural depression between the Cathedral/ Fountain Court area and the Artemis Temple complex; it probably reached down to the Nymphaeum, where its entrance into the Cardo may have been a smaller passageway than the upper street that has been cleared at this point. On the right, as you walk up the Stepped Street, is a reconstructed vault under the south side of the Artemis Temple *temenos*. This was made into a public museum in the 1950s, but is now temporarily closed to the public because it has had to serve as a storehouse for many of the mosaics and archaeological artefacts that have been excavated at Jerash during the past half century.

THE BATHS OF PLACCUS

The area to your left as you walk up the Stepped Street, bounded to the east by the Sarapion Passage, was excavated in 1931 by an American team led by C.S. Fisher, but retains little interest for the visitor today. Inscriptions found here confirm that this was a public baths complex from the Byzantine period, built by Bishop Placcus in 454–5 and restored in 584. Entered from the Stepped

Street via an open portico of six re-used Corinthian columns, the baths covered an area of some 22.5 by 41 metres. Around a large central *atrium* was a complex of many rooms that corresponded to the standard layout of earlier Roman baths. The complex included a 4.5-metre-square *tepidarium* with a shallow basin; two *caldaria* with cement bath tubs; a large, 1.32-metre-deep swimming pool; changing rooms; and latrines. Excavated artefacts included pieces of marble statuary, coins, pottery, tools, glass fragments and a tripedal bronze jug.

This Byzantine baths complex, along with another that has been excavated at Umm Qais (Gadara) in north Jordan, shows the continuity of the public bath from Roman, through Byzantine, and into the Umayyad years, the latter being best represented in Jordan by the baths at Qasr Amra, near Azraq. The Baths of Placcus are considerably smaller than the great East and West Baths of Roman Jerash, but they are interesting because they were built by a bishop in the midst of an important religious precinct within the centre of the city. They would have formed a logical part of the *domus ecclesiae* (the greater house) that was the larger precinct in which the *domus Dei* (the house of God) was located. The *domus ecclesiae* often included many public buildings of a purely secular nature, such as baths, schools or hospitals.

THE CLERGY HOUSE

Immediately beyond the Baths of Placcus, on the same side of the street, is an area excavated in 1931 but subsequently largely reburied. Here was a complicated, overlapping series of otherwise ordinary rooms and walls that were frequently expanded and changed over time, attesting to the use of this part of the city from its earliest days. After the Church of St Theodore was built in 495, this area served as the 'Clergy House', in Kraeling's words, housing some of the clergy of the church and probably the bishop as well. The original house was simply laid out, with two groups of rooms on either side of a central courtyard. It was entered from the south, through a door facing the *atrium* of the Church of St Theodore. The interior was rearranged several times, with new rooms, corridors and entrances being created, often at the expense of the courtyard space. Some of the walls of the Clergy House stood on the remains of 2nd or 3rd-century AD Roman structures, particularly evident just to the north, on the line of the Stepped Street. Excavations below some of the rooms of the Clergy House turned up even earlier occupation levels, in the form of caves whose roofs had collapsed under the weight of later construction. Kraeling suggested that these caves formed part of the 1st or 2nd-century AD early Roman cemetery that covered areas of the south slope of the city's upper terrace.

THE CHURCH OF ST THEODORE

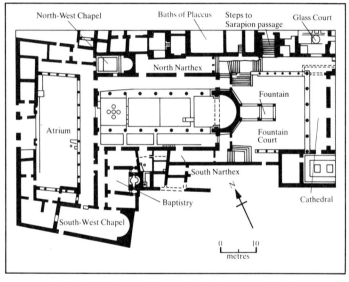

The Church of St Theodore, AD 494–6 *(after A.G. Buchanan and C.S. Fisher)*

On a terrace five metres above and immediately west of the Fountain Court is the Church of St Theodore. Inscriptions tell us that its foundations were laid in 494, under the authority of a certain Bishop Aeneas, and that it was dedicated in 496. The base of the polygon-shaped apse of the new church projected right into the Fountain Court, obliterating the court's western colonnade and some columns from both the north and south colonnades. A flight of steps at the north-west corner of the Fountain Court leads up to the level of the church. From passageways and adjoining rooms along the north and south sides of the church, three or four doors led respectively into the nave; the other entrances consisted of three doors in the west wall, and two doors passing into the east end of the two aisles from small rooms flanking the apse.

The Church of St Theodore

The body of the church is divided into a nave and two side aisles by two rows of seven Corinthian columns; these, like the construction materials for most of the rest of the church, were re-used from earlier Roman buildings of the 2nd or 3rd century AD. Arches springing from the colonnade supported a wall which in turn supported a timber and tile roof. A half-dome over the apse was covered with sparkling glass mosaics, contributing to the richness of the internal decoration which also included patterned and coloured marble and stone slab paving for the floor of the nave and aisles, marble-clad walls, and generous use of glass mosaics in the upper reaches of the walls. A chancel screen across the nave between the first two columns marked off the raised chancel and altar area, from which the *ambo*, or pulpit, projected westwards slightly into the nave.

West of the body of the church was the rhomboid-shaped atrium. Measuring about 30 metres by 10 metres, it spanned the west wall of the church as well as the adjacent baptistry and its two flanking rooms. From a small street to the west of the *atrium*, a triple entrance (of which the central door only remains open) led into a small hall with mosaic floors, flanked to the north and south by three rooms with mosaic floors. From here, three long steps, flanked by internal niches originally built as thrones or seats, descended into the *atrium*'s open courtyard. Porticoes on the north, east and south sides of the courtyard were composed of Ionic columns, below which were floors covered with mosaics. To the north of the courtyard were three rooms partly cut out of the rock, beyond which was the Clergy House. To the east of these rooms was a small chapel with a fine mosaic floor, with doors from the *atrium* and from the north aisle of the church. Outside the south-west corner of the church was a series of rooms with mosaic floors, which led in turn into a baptistry. The baptistry, with a small oval pool–font in its eastern apse, seems to have been rebuilt over an earlier chapel whose floor level was one foot lower than the baptistry floor. East of the baptistry are three rooms with mosaic floors that may have been living quarters for the clergy. A passage west of the baptistry led southwards to the South-West Chapel, with its own small *atrium* to the west, limestone and marble floor paving, an apse and a chancel area and screen.

THE CHURCHES OF SS COSMAS AND DAMIAN, ST JOHN THE BAPTIST AND ST GEORGE

Some 150 metres west-north-west of the Church of St Theodore is an integrated group of three early 6th-century churches that shared a common *atrium* and connected with one another through internal doors. They are reached today by a sloping track heading south-west from the Temple of Artemis. They are the Church of St John the Baptist, in the centre, flanked to the left by the Church of SS Cosmas and Damian, and to the right by the Church of St George. All three were built between 529 and 533. They were excavated in 1929 by A.H.M. Jones, and were studied by F.M. Biebel and J.W. Crowfoot.

The churches can be viewed today from the north, from above a modern protective wall. This aerial perspective gives a good view of the common west *atrium* that the three churches shared. It had a colonnade of fourteen Corinthian columns on a low stylobate, though only the columns on the east side of the *atrium* remain today. The area between the columns and the church entrances was once paved with red and white mosaics, with different patterns in front of each church. The floor of the *atrium* itself, west of the surviving colonnade, was paved with stone slabs.

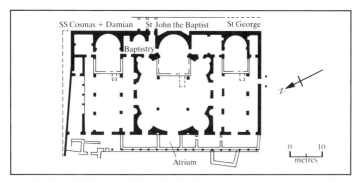

The Churches of SS Cosmas and Damian, St John the Baptist, and St George (*after C.S. Fisher*)

The Church of SS Cosmas and Damian, which includes the best preserved mosaics in Jerash, is composed of a half-domed apse, and a central nave separated from its north and south aisles by two rows of solid piers. A noteworthy architectural feature is the *exedra*, or open recess, north of the north aisle and separated from it by an open colonnade of three Corinthian columns. This area, with its coarse red and white mosaic floor, may also have been a *narthex*, a long, arcaded porch often found in early Christian churches, though usually situated before the main entrance. The chancel area and altar were delineated by a chancel screen across the nave at the first row of piers, from which a pulpit supported on three small columns projected slightly into the nave. The apse was flanked by a small square room to the north, and to the south by a baptistry with an apse that also opened into the adjacent Church of St John the Baptist. This baptistry was first laid out as a chapel, with a chancel screen in front of the apse and two flanking chambers covered with mosaic floors. Three doors led into the church nave and aisles from the *atrium* to the west, with a fourth door leading into the *exedra*.

The church was dedicated to the twin brothers Cosmas and Damian, respectively the patrons of medicine and pharmacy.

They were born in Arabia, studied medicine in Syria, and finally were martyred during the reign of the Roman Emperor Diocletian just before AD 305. Their devotion to God and to their profession, combined with their legendary service to the poor and the sick, brought them a reputation as miraculous healers; and, since the 6th century, shrines, memorials and churches have been erected in their honour.

Detail of mosaic paving in the Church of SS Cosmas and Damian

The huge mosaic covering the floor of the nave is especially noteworthy. It consists of alternating diamonds and squares with geometric designs, many pictures of birds and animals, and some portraits of donors in the first row of diamonds. At the top of the mosaic, immediately below the chancel screen, is a mosaic inscription dedicating the church to the twin brothers Saints Cosmas and Damian; it also gives the date of the church as 533 and the name of the patron as Bishop Paul. It is flanked by portraits of Theodore the *paramonarius*, or the church warden (to the left), and his wife Georgia, with her hands extended in prayer (to the right). Below the portrait of Georgia are the stubs of the three small columns that held up the *ambo*, or pulpit. The floors of the aisles were covered with a simpler geometric pattern.

The central, and largest, of the three churches in this complex is the **Church of St John the Baptist**, completed in 531 under the patronage of Bishop Paul. It consisted of a circular internal plan set inside a square, with four horseshoe-shaped *exedrae* at the four corners of the square, and a similarly horseshoe-shaped apse surrounded by seats in the east end. A.H.M. Jones notes that this peculiar layout, measuring 29.5 by 23.8 metres, was a smaller version of the cathedral at Bostra, built about twenty years earlier in 512–13. To the north of the apse was the baptistry that also opened into the Church of SS Cosmas and Damian; to the south was a long room, presumably a sacristy, that also gave access to and served the adjacent Church of St George. Most of the stones for the church were re-used from abandoned earlier Roman buildings, including the Temple of Zeus. The four Corinthian columns forming a square in the middle of the church are re-used 2nd-century AD columns. The four *exedrae* and the large apse carried semi-domes that were brightly decorated with glass mosaics, while fine plastering, stone and marble covered the internal walls. The church was entered from the *atrium* to the west through three doors, the two on the outside giving into the western *exedrae*. A possible window over the main doorway may have been designed to admit light into the church. The chancel area reached from the apse to the first pair of columns.

Little remains today of the fine mosaic pavement that originally covered the nave of the church, though it was studied and partly preserved in 1929. It included panels with personifications of the months and seasons, a grape-vine trellis, animals, birds, human portraits, acanthus borders, Maltese crosses, fantastic candelabra, and floral patterns. Particularly noteworthy were the representations of several cities and shrines in Egypt, of special significance as religious and pilgrimage centres, often in river landscapes with jumping fish, ducks, storks and herons. Some of the sites depicted were Alexandria, Pharos, Canopus, and Memphis, along with the shrine of SS John and Cyrus at Menuthis. Most of the mosaics that were preserved have been locked away for safe keeping.

The Church of St George was the first of these three churches to be completed, in 529–30. It is a basilical church, almost identical in plan and size to the Church of SS Cosmas and

Damian, and has the same three pairs of internal piers carrying the roof and dividing the interior of the church into a central nave and two side aisles. The church was entered through three doors from the *atrium* to the west and a door that gave onto a porch to the south. A window may have been located above the central door in the west wall. A chancel screen crossed the nave at the line of the first pair of piers, and seats for the clergy went around the inside of the apse. The apse was flanked by two rooms, both presumably sacristies where the church's holy artefacts were kept.

There is some evidence to suggest that the Church of St George continued in use for a time after the other two churches were abandoned and robbed of much of their contents. J.W. Crowfoot suggests they were badly damaged by an earthquake in the 7th or early 8th century (perhaps the earthquake of 747), after which only the Church of St George and the baptistry continued in use, while the other two churches were abandoned. There are some who believe that St George's Church may have served as the cathedral of Jerash in the 8th century. This theory is partly substantiated by the state of the mosaics in the three churches. Those in St George's and St John's were disfigured following the iconoclastic decree of the Umayyad Caliph Yazid II (720–24), who decreed that 'all images and likenesses in his dominions, of bronze, and of wood and of stone and of pigments, should be destroyed'. The human and animal pictures in the mosaics of St George's and St John's, as in almost all the mosaics of Jordan at the time, were destroyed and replaced with plain or geometric patterns. But the mosaic floor of the Church of SS Cosmas and Damian was spared, perhaps because it had already been abandoned or even partly covered with rubble in 720, and therefore escaped the eye of the iconoclasts.

The mosaics of the Church of St George included the large floor mosaic in the nave, with its cross, hexagon and octagon pattern filled in with human and animal portraits and floral decorations. The north and south aisles had assorted geometric and floral patterns with human and animal representations.

THE SYNAGOGUE CHURCH

On high ground overlooking the Temple of Artemis from the

The Synagogue Church, looking west

west are the ruins of the Synagogue Church, so called because the 6th-century church was built over an earlier, 3rd or 4th-century AD building that is thought to have been a synagogue. The atrium was to the east of the building because the synagogue itself would have faced the temple in Jerusalem, to the west. The atrium had Corinthian columns on square, pulvinated pedestals, which appear in a few other buildings in Jerash, Hisban and Galilee.

The synagogue seems to have been composed of a vestibule, a nave and two side aisles, an *ambo*, and perhaps a projecting chamber to the west. Mosaic floor remains include representations of the story of the Flood with pictures of men and animals, and an inscription giving the names of the three benefactors who repaired the synagogue some time after it was first built: 'Phinehas son of Baruch, Jose son of Samuel and Yudan son of Hezekiah.' It has been suggested that the presence of the synagogue here marks this as the ancient Jewish quarter of the city, with the location of the synagogue on one of the highest points of the city perhaps reflecting the Jewish belief that a city whose rooftops overlook the synagogue is destined for destruction.

When the Byzantine church was built on the same site in 530–31, under the aegis of Bishop Paul, the entire east–west orientation of the building had to be reversed. The Christian builders removed some structures from the west end of the former synagogue, raised the entire floor level, and redesigned the eastern part to conform to the standard layout of a Byzantine church. The west colonnade of the former *atrium* was removed to make room for the new apse, which was flanked by two doors giving access to the two aisles from the *atrium*. There was also a single door in the centre of the west wall. The central nave was separated from the side aisles by the synagogue's two original colonnades, each with seven columns, but an extra pair of columns was added at the east end to support the roof over the chancel area. The nave and aisles were repaved with mosaics whose human and animal representations were later disfigured in the early 8th century. One step led up from the nave to the chancel and altar area between the first two columns from the east. The marble-clad *ambo* was located in the usual area, projecting into the nave from the chancel screen; the altar was within the apse.

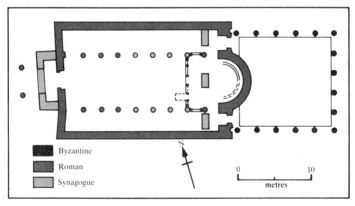

The Synagogue Church (*after C.S. Fisher*)

THE CHURCH OF BISHOP GENESIUS

About fifty metres west of the three churches of SS Cosmas and Damian, St John the Baptist and St George, are the ruins of the Church of Bishop Genesius, studied in 1929 by J.W. Crowfoot. A mosaic floor inscription dates it to 611, making it the last Christian church to be built in the city, just a few years before the Persian invasion. It was built during the episcopate of Bishop

Genesius, though to whom the church was dedicated is not known. It is a basilical church with a central nave separated from the side aisles by two rows of seven columns; from the columns, arches sprang to support a wall, which in turn supported the roof. A single external apse had no flanking side rooms; instead, at the eastern end of the two aisles, were two small chapels with niches in their eastern walls and their own chancel screens that lined up with the main chancel screen of the church.

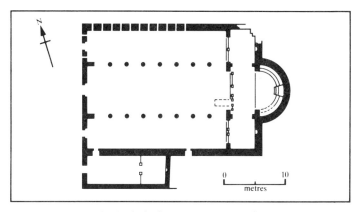

The Church of Bishop Genesius (*after C.S. Fisher*)

The raised chancel screen is the only one in Jerash which runs across the full width of the nave and aisles of the church. This became a standard feature in later Greek Orthodox churches. Two semicircular rows of seats for the clergy ran along the inside of the apse, interrupted in the middle by a small flight of steps leading up to the bishop's seat. The altar was located directly in front of the bishop's seat, while the *ambo* projected slightly into the nave from the chancel screen. The rather substantial foundations of the chancel screen may have carried a heavier, more elaborate, columned screen typical of some post-Byzantine Greek churches, rather than the standard low screen of earlier Byzantine churches.

The nave, aisle, and chancel floors were covered with mosaics, and marble once covered the walls of the apse. Three doors led into the church from the west, where there are traces of an external *atrium* that has never been excavated. A fourth door

The Church of Bishop Genesius

from the west gave into a chapel outside the south-west corner of the church, with a mosaic-paved nave, a raised, mosaic-paved chancel, and a small niche in the east wall instead of an apse.

THE CHURCH OF SS PETER AND PAUL

In the south-west corner of the city, just a few metres away from the city walls, are the ruins of the Church of SS Peter and Paul, excavated in 1929 under the supervision of J.W. Crowfoot. No inscriptions have been found that give its precise date, but parallels in its architecture and mosaics with other dated churches in the city place its construction around 540. A mosaic inscription in the church says it was built by the 'famed Anastasius, who teaches the trustworthy things of divine inspiration', and was dedicated to 'the first of the Apostles, Peter and Paul'. Anastasius is assumed to be the bishop who followed Paul as the Bishop of Gerasa.

This basilical church followed the standard pattern of a central nave separated from two side aisles by colonnades of eight re-used 2nd or 3rd-century AD Corinthian columns. The apse is flanked by two small chapels with niches in their eastern walls. Two rows of clergy-seats around the marble or limestone-clad apse are well preserved, with a raised seat in the centre for the bishop. A stone block with three parallel slots in it now balances on its side in front of the apse; this was the base for a Calvary, a chapel surmounted by a cross, that stood directly in front of the Bishop's seat. The altar and chancel area in front of the apse ended with the chancel screen at the second pair of columns in the nave, from which the *ambo* projected slightly into the nave. The solid chancel screen of the side chapels reached only the first columns, so the side chapels were entered from in front of the apse, and not directly from the side aisles. The apse ceiling was richly decorated with coloured glass mosaics, the side chapels with simpler white mosaics.

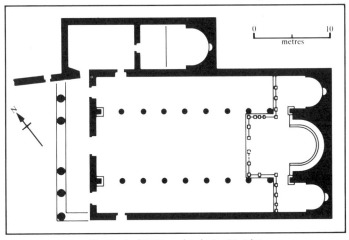

The Church of SS Peter and Paul (*after C.S. Fisher*)

A colonnaded *atrium* to the west, with a paved and mosaic-decorated floor, led through three main doors into the nave and aisles. Another door led north from the *atrium* into the anteroom of the small chapel built on the north-west corner of the church. The chapel, which also communicated with the north aisle through a door, had the usual apse with a small niche, a chancel and chancel screen, and the anteroom to the west. A wall along the north end of the *atrium* had two doors, the larger of which was flanked by two niches and seems to have been the main entrance into this religious 'precinct'.

130

The Church of SS Peter and Paul

The church's mosaics, now removed or covered, included a nave mosaic divided into several sections, similar to the arrangement in the Church of St John the Baptist. Here also were representations of cities such as Alexandria and Memphis, an acanthus border, animals, floral patterns, personifications of the four seasons, and geometric designs.

Before the church was abandoned, its mosaic floor was repaired in places and a new low bench was constructed against the west wall. Later yet, most likely in the 8th century, the three doors in the west wall were blocked up, and walls were built in the external *atrium* which was converted for non-religious, probably domestic, uses.

THE MORTUARY CHURCH

About fifteen metres south of the Church of SS Peter and Paul are the remains of the small Mortuary Church, tucked into the hillside on which the city wall also stands. A mosaic inscription in the nave says the unnamed founder of the church built it in honour of his parents, who may well have been buried in the cave inside the south wall. The precise date of the church is not known, but has been placed towards the end of the 6th century, according to the

The Mortuary Church

mosaic evidence. This 'single hall church', as Crowfoot called it when he excavated it in 1929, was entered through a main door in the north wall, from which steps led up to the mosaic-paved nave.

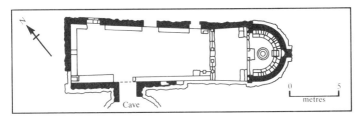

The Mortuary Church (*after C.S. Fisher*)

Its eastern apse had a large niche, and was covered by a half-dome. The surviving arch in the south wall led to an underground burial cave. A chancel screen with a central door ran across the front of the nave, separating it from the mosaic-paved chancel and altar area. The chancel screen projected into the nave along the south wall, perhaps where the *ambo* stood. A double row of seats runs around the inside of the apse, whose floor was paved with marble. The mosaics of the Mortuary Church were in poor condition, and had been patched up with large pieces of stone and marble, presumably after the iconoclastic movement of the early 8th century had removed all human and animal representations.

GROUP 8

THE EAST BATHS

The East Baths are one of the few remains of ancient public buildings on the east bank of the River Chrysorhoas, and indicate that even though there was some civic development in that part of the ancient city, it was considerably less important than the west side of the city. The East Baths are rather lost and ravaged today among the bustle of the modern town of Jerash. But in an ironic way, this may help recall the setting of the baths in ancient days, for it is generally assumed by most archaeologists and other scholars who have studied Jerash that the east bank of the river was largely an area of domestic houses and villas, not very much unlike the modern development of the city. Certainly, such a huge and perhaps even stately building would not have been hemmed in by other structures and streets as its surviving ruins are today. But its setting today reminds us that these were, after all, utilitarian buildings that would have served hundreds or perhaps even thousands of people every day, particularly during the hot summer months. For all its past grandeur and enormous size (it was even bigger than the West Baths), we know very little about the East Baths building. Mr C.S. Fisher says, in the Kraeling study, that the baths once had four large chambers, the largest of which measured 27 by 13 metres and had walls five metres thick. A room to its south measured at least 18 by 9.5 metres, and two other rooms to the west included, respectively, semicircular entrance niches and heavy corner piers joined by a large arch that still stands today.

The East Baths

THE CHURCH OF PROCOPIUS

This is another of the few buildings whose remains can be seen on the east bank of the city. It sits atop a high hill not far from the eastern city wall, almost directly due east from the South Tetrakionion and the South Bridge. A mosaic floor inscription says the church was built in 526–7, making it the first of the churches built in the city in the 6th century. It was established under the supervision of an officer named Procopius, in the days of the Bishop Paul, but we do not know to whom it was dedicated. It is a basilical church with a nave separated from two side aisles by two colonnades, each of six Corinthian columns. Little remains to be seen of the church today, other than the column bases and some drums, for the floor mosaics and the eastern apse and wall that were excavated in 1928 were later reburied. The church would have been entered through three doors in the west wall. A door in the north-west corner led into the adjacent north chapel. The apse was surrounded by two tiers of seats, and its plaster was painted to resemble red-veined marble. The central apse was flanked by two smaller apses with plastered walls. A chancel screen crossed the nave at the level of the second pair of columns, and independent chancel screens separated the side apses from the aisles.

The church once sported a rich collection of floor mosaics which were defaced but later repaired; the nave mosaic was one of

134

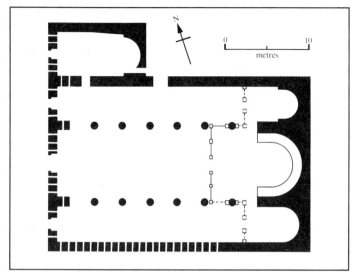

The Church of Procopius (*after A.G. Buchanan and C.S. Fisher*)

the city's finest. Among the elements in the mosaics of the nave, aisles and side chapels were an acanthus border, animals, baskets of grapes or flowers, trees and bushes, geometric patterns, human representations, chalices, and interlacing circles with rainbow patterns.

GROUP 9

BIRKETEIN RESERVOIR AND FESTIVAL THEATRE

About 200 metres north of the North Gate on the paved road to Birketein, you will see on your right a recently cleared building with many standing columns. This is a Byzantine church with an octagonal east side, similar to the octagonal church excavated at Umm Qais, in north Jordan. The church has Ionic columns on its north and south sides, and monolithic Corinthian columns on its east and west sides, with granite columns in the octagonal area. The church was cleared and partly excavated in early 1983, but has not been fully studied. It may stand on the remains of an earlier Roman building, perhaps even the Roman Temple of Nemesis which is known from inscriptional evidence to have been located in this area.

The area of the Birketein reservoir and Festival Theatre lies 1500 metres due north of the North Gate, in a small, well watered valley surrounded by many trees and filled with the peculiar combination of the voices of birds and frogs. The area may have been Gerasa's 'semi-sacred pleasure ground', as C.C. McCown called it in the 1930s, where annual festivals were celebrated through the pagan and Christian eras. An inscription discovered here confirms it as the site of the annual Maiuma Festivals, mentioned by Christian and non-Christian writers from the 4th century onwards. The nautical festivals, in which naked women participated, appear to have taken rather promiscuous turns, and were banned and reinstated several times during the Byzantine period.

'Birketein' in Arabic means 'two pools' or 'double pool'. The rectangular pool, which flares slightly at the south-east corner, measures 88.5 by 43.5 metres, and is three metres deep. It is divided into two parts by a 2.8-metre-thick wall 18 metres from its southern end, in which a sluice gate regulated the level of water in the larger northern pool. Stones projecting from the wall into the pool at irregular intervals provided standing places for people to draw water.

A processional way ran northwards from the city to Birketein, opening into a gateway just off the south-western corner of the pool. The way then passed alongside a colonnade along the western length of the pool, and continued northward to the vicinity of the Tomb of Germanus. The colonnade may have surrounded the entire pool in antiquity, according to Mr C.C. McCown who excavated the complex in the early 1930s.

The Festival Theatre, south-west of the pool, directly overlooks its southern portion. It was built into the side of a steep hill, about eight metres above the level of the processional way but slightly off axis from the pool itself. Steps led up to the theatre through two arched entrances, or *paradoi*, at either end of the stage. The small theatre could probably have accommodated up

The Festival Theatre at Birketein

to 1000 spectators in its *cavea*, which was divided into four equal sections by stepped aisles. Architectural evidence further up the hill suggests the theatre may have had an upper section, which would have doubled its present size. The wood-covered stage was 25.8 metres long and just 4.6 metres wide, separated from the audience by a 12-metre-wide orchestra paved with stone slabs.

The *scaenae frons*, the wall at the back of the stage, is enigmatic, for only its foundations remain. Some scholars argue the *scaenae frons* never existed, to allow the spectators an unobstructed view of the festivities in the pool, but the more widely accepted interpretation is that the Festival Theatre had a rather simple, solid and lightly decorated *scaenae frons*.

Inscriptions date the Birketein pool and Festival Theatre to the late 2nd or early 3rd century, with the pool's west colonnade firmly dated to AD 209–11.

THE TOMB OF GERMANUS

Just over 100 metres north of the Birketein pool are the ruins of the Tomb of Germanus, probably dating from the Antonine period in the middle of the 2nd century AD. This is a Roman 'temple-type' tomb with a four-pillared portico leading into a square *cella*. The tumbled stones and the open sarcophagus lie silently around the three remaining standing pillars still holding up their entablature, virtually in the same position in which they fell hundreds of years ago.

This is most likely the tomb of the same wealthy, civic-minded Germanus, son of Molpon, a Centurion of an auxiliary cohort, who financed the reconstruction of the Temple of Zeus Epicarpius (the 'fruit bearer'). This now vanished temple is known only from an inscription fragment found on the site at the turn of the century.

The Tomb of Germanus

Selected Bibliography of Books and Articles

Barghouti, Asem N. 'Urbanization of Palestine and Jordan in Hellenistic and Roman Times,' A. Hadidi (ed.) *Studies in the History and Archaeology of Jordan I,* Department of Antiquities of the Hashemite Kingdom of Jordan, Amman (1982) pp. 209–30.

Bellinger, A.R. 'The Early Coinage of Roman Syria,' *Studies in Roman Economic and Social History in Honour of A.C. Johnson,* Princeton (1951).

Beitenhard, H. 'Die Dekapolis von Pompeius bis Trajan', *Aufstieg und Niedergang der Romischen Welt II.8 (1977).*

Bowersock, G.W. *Roman Arabia,* Harvard University Press, Cambridge and London (1983).

'Syria Under Vespasian,' *Journal of Roman Studies 63* (1973) pp. 133–40.

'A Report on Provincia Arabia,' *Journal of Roman Studies 63* (1973) pp. 219–42.

'Limes Arabicus,' *Harvard Studies in Classical Philology 80* (1976) pp. 219–29.

Browning, I. *Jerash and the Decapolis,* Chatto and Windus, London (1982).

Brunnow, R.E. and Domaszewski, A. *Die Provincia Arabia* (3 vols.), Strasbourg (1904–9).

Casson, L. 'Rome's Trade with the East: The Sea Voyage to Africa and India,' *Transactions of the American Philological Association 110* (1980) pp. 21–36.

Cumont, F. 'Frontier Provinces of the East,' *Cambridge Ancient History* (1936) vol. 11, pp. 613–48.

Dudley, D. *Roman Society,* Penguin, London (1975).

Graf, D.F. 'Saracens and the Defence of the Arabian Frontier,' *Bulletin of the American Schools of Oriental Research 229* (1978) pp. 1–26.

'A Preliminary Report on a Survey of Nabataean–Roman Military Sites in Southern Jordan,' *Annual of the Department of Antiquities of Jordan 23* (1979) pp. 121–7.

Grant, M. *History of Rome,* Faber and Faber, London and Boston (1978).

Harding, G.L. 'Recent Work on the Jerash Forum,' *Palestine Exploration Quarterly* (1949) pp. 12–20.

The Antiquities of Jordan, Lutterworth Press, London (1974).

Isaac, B. 'The Decapolis in Syria, a Neglected Inscription,' *Zeitschrift für Papyrologie und Epigraphik 44* (1981) pp. 67–74.

Jones, A.H.M. *The Greek City, from Alexander to Justinian,* The Clarendon Press, Oxford (1940).

The Cities of the Eastern Roman Provinces, The Clarendon Press, Oxford (1971).

Kennedy, D.L. 'The Frontier Policy of Septimius Severus: New Evidence from Arabia', W.S. Hanson and L.J.F. Keppie (eds.) *Roman Frontier Studies 12* (1979) pp. 879–88.

'Legio VI Ferrata: The Annexation and Early Garrison of Arabia', *Harvard Studies in Classical Philology 84* (1980) pp. 283–309.

'Archaeological Explorations on the Roman Frontier in Northeast Jordan, the Roman and Byzantine Military Installations and Road Network on the Ground and from the Air,' *BAR International Series 134*, Oxford (1982).

Kirkbride, D. 'Notes on a survey of pre-Roman archaeological sites near Jerash,' *Bulletin of the Institute of Archaeology I*, University of London (1958) pp. 9–20.

Kraeling, C.H. (ed.) *Gerasa: City of the Decapolis*, American Schools of Oriental Research, New Haven (1938).

Lewis, N. and Reinhold, M. (eds.) *Roman Civilisation, Sourcebook II: The Empire*, Harper and Row, New York (1955).

Lyttelton, M. *Baroque Architecture in Classical Antiquity*, London (1974).

Mittman, S. 'The Roman Road from Gerasa to Adraa,' *Annual of the Department of Antiquities of Jordan 11* (1966) pp. 65–87.

Parapetti, R. 'The Architectural Significance of the Sanctuary of Artemis at Gerasa,' A. Hadidi (ed.) *Studies in the History and Archaeology of Jordan I*, Department of Antiquities of the Hashemite Kingdom of Jordan, Amman (1982) pp. 255–60.

Parker, S.T. 'The Decapolis Reviewed,' *Journal of Biblical Literature* (1975) pp. 431–7.

'Towards a History of the Limes Arabicus,' Hanson and Keppie (eds.) *Roman Frontier Studies 12*, London (1980) pp. 865–78.

Raschke, M. 'New Studies in Roman Commerce with the East,' *Aufstieg und Niedergang der Romischen Welt II.9.2* (1978) pp. 604–1361.

Runciman, S. *Byzantine Style and Civilization*, Penguin, London (1975).

Seyrig, H. 'Temples, Cultes et Souvenirs Historiques de la Decapole,' *Syria 36* (1959) pp. 60–78.

Smith, R.H. *Pella of the Decapolis*, The College of Wooster (1973).

Spijkerman, A. M. Piccirillo (ed.) *The Coins of the Decapolis and Provincia Arabia*, Franciscan Press, Jerusalem (1978).

Ward-Perkins, J.B. *Roman Imperial Architecture*, Penguin, London (1981).

Glossary

ambo: stand raised on steps and used for readings in church
architrave: lowest of the three main parts of entablature
atrium: open court in front of church
boulé: city council (hence bouleterion = council chamber)
cardo: main, usually north–south, street in typical ancient city plan
cavea: auditorium or rows of seating in theatre
cella: main body of temple, containing cult image
chancel: part of east end of church, containing main altar
colonnade: row of columns carrying entablature or arches
Corinthian: one of the 'orders' of classical architecture based on a column type; developed from Ionic order
crypta: (usually) underground passage
decumanus: main east–west street in city plan
diaconicon: room in church for receiving congregation's offerings (often also served as vestry and library)
entablature: upper part of an order, consisting of architrave, frieze and cornice
exedra: semicircular or rectangular recess with raised seats
Ionic: architectural order, preceding Corinthian
narthex: vestibule, usually preceding nave and aisle or facade
odeon (*Latin 'odeum'*):   small theatre, usually roofed
parados: lateral entrance on to orchestra and stage of theatre
pediment: gable above portico
peristyle: range of columns surrounding building or open court
pilaster: shallow rectangular column projecting slightly from wall
portico: roofed space forming entrance of facade of church
propylaeum (*plural 'propylaea'*):   entrance gateway to enclosure, usually of temple
scaena: stage building of theatre
stylobate: base on which colonnade stands
temenos: sacred precinct or enclosure
tetrakionion (*Latin 'quadrifons'*):   pavilion structure built on four columns, or four such pavilions placed at intersecting streets
tetrapylon: four arches joining each other to form a square, usually roofed
tribunalium: raised platform with seating for officials and dignitaries
velarium: awning or screen drawn across theatre
vomitorium: entrance to theatre

Index

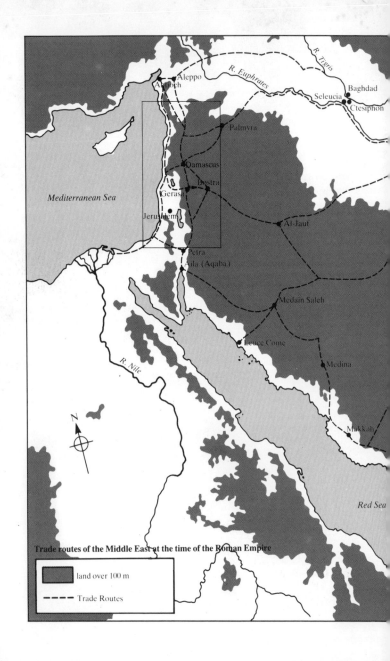

Trade routes of the Middle East at the time of the Roman Empire

land over 100 m

---- Trade Routes